BA...

TRAVEL GUIDE
2025

Explore Germany's Heartland, from Alpine Peaks to Historic Castles, Bavarian Culture, and Practical Tips for Visitors

Donald M. Clark

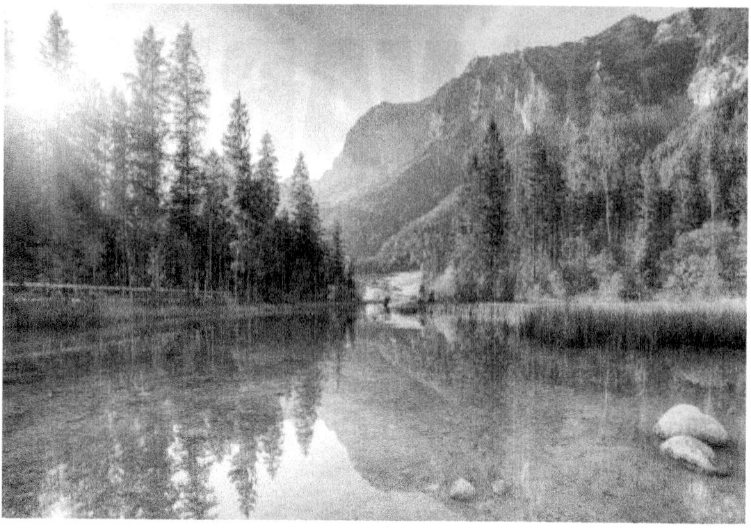

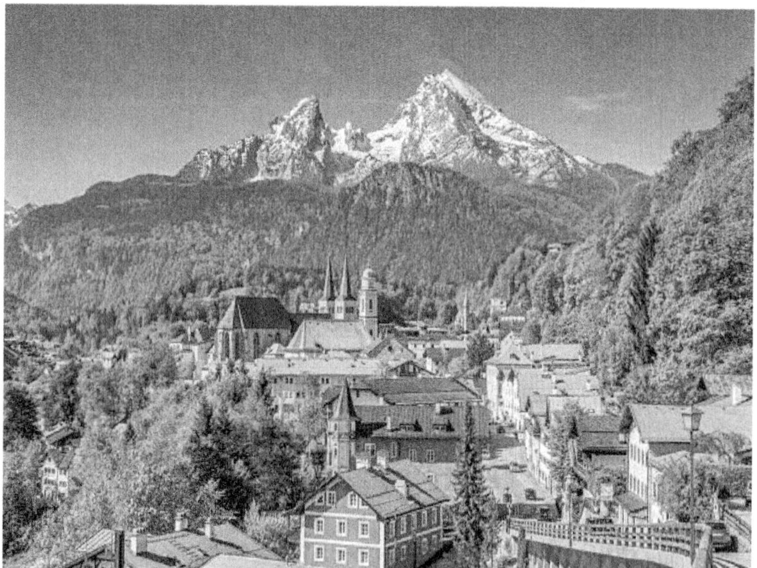

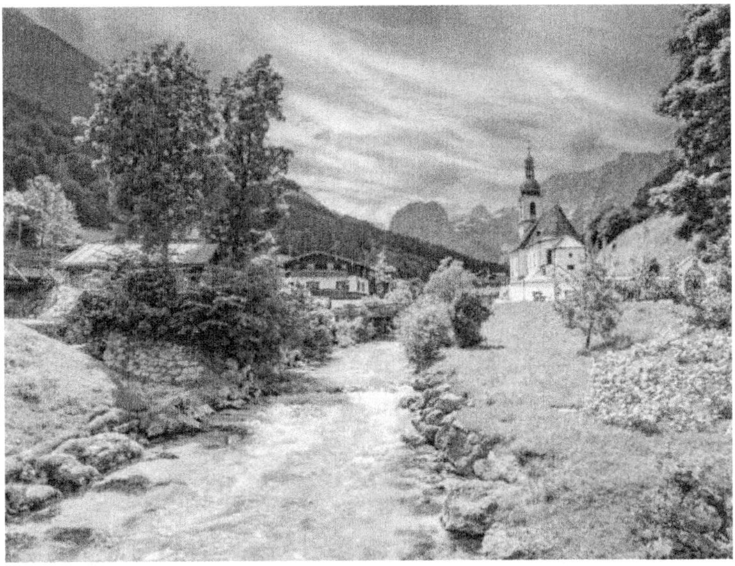

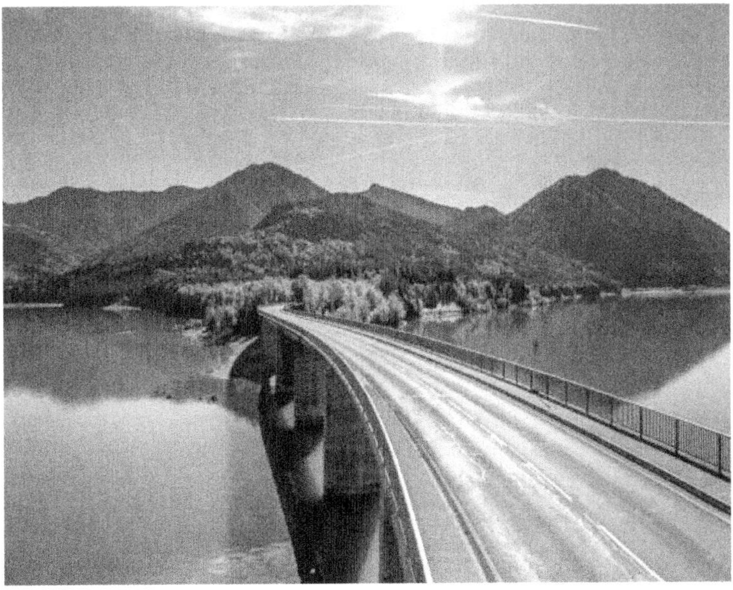

All rights reserved. No part of this publication may be reproduced, distributed, or transmitted in any form or by any means, including photocopying, recording, or other electronic or mechanical methods, without the prior written permission of the publisher, except in the case of brief quotations embodied in critical reviews and certain other noncommercial uses permitted by copyright law.

Copyright ©Donald M. Clark, 2025.

Table Of Content

MAP OF BAVARIA..6
Chapter 1: Introduction to Bavaria...................7
  Overview of Bavaria..7
  Why Visit Bavaria?..10
  Best Time to Visit Bavaria................................13
  Getting to Bavaria...16
  Language & Communication............................20
Chapter 2: Planning Your Trip to Bavaria......**25**
  Budgeting and Cost of Travel........................... 25
  Accommodation Options...................................29
  Transportation Within Bavaria.........................32
  Safety Tips and Emergency Information.........35
  Cultural Etiquette and Local Customs............. 40
Chapter 3: Must-See Destinations in Bavaria..**44**
  Munich The Heart of Bavaria........................... 44
  Neuschwanstein Castle.................................... 49
  The Bavarian Alps.. 52
  Nuremberg Medieval Charm............................56
  Regensburg & Bamberg................................... 59
Chapter 4: Bavarian Culture and Traditions......**64**
  Oktoberfest.. 64
  Bavarian Cuisine...69
  Folk Traditions and Festivals........................... 73
  The Bavarian Dialect.. 77
  Crafts, Art, and Souvenirs................................81
Chapter 5: Outdoor Adventures and Natural Beauty..

4

Hiking in the Bavarian Alps...................................84
Cycling In Bavaria..92
Bavarian Lakes and Water Activities...................... 96
Winter Activities in the Alps................................. 100
Wildlife and Nature Reserves............................... 104
Chapter 6: Shopping and Souvenirs.......................110
Shopping in Munich and Nuremberg.................... 110
Bavarian Marketplaces... 113
Traditional Clothing and Apparel...........................118
Gifts and Gourmet Delights.................................. 121
Chapter 7: Practical Information and Tips............. 125
Local Laws and Regulations.................................125
Money, Currency and Banking..............................130
Emergency Contacts and Useful Numbers...........133
Essential Travel Apps and Websites.................... 137
Chapter 8: Suggested Itinerary for Bavaria............142
3-Day Itinerary for First-Time Visitors................... 142
7-Day Itinerary for a Deeper Exploration of Bavaria... 145
Conclusion.. 149

MAP OF BAVARIA

Chapter 1: Introduction to Bavaria

Overview of Bavaria

Bavaria, located in southeastern Germany, is one of the country's most beautiful and culturally rich areas. It is surrounded by Austria to the south, the Czech Republic to the east, and other German states such as Baden-Württemberg and Hesse. It is Germany's largest state, covering around 70,000 square kilometers and accounting for nearly one-fifth of the total land area. Bavaria has a population of almost 13 million, making it Germany's second-most populated state after North Rhine-Westphalia.

When I first arrived in Bavaria, I was astonished by the landscape's incredible diversity. From the spectacular peaks of the Bavarian Alps in the south, which are ideal for skiing in the winter and trekking in the summer, to the rolling hills and verdant valleys, there is so much to see. The region's natural beauty is enhanced by its historical cities, beautiful towns, and picturesque villages, making it a popular destination for both tourists and locals.

Bavaria's prominence in Germany goes much beyond its size and population. It is well-known for its cultural, historical, and traditional significance. Many of Germany's most recognizable icons, such as beer culture, fairy-tale castles, and Oktoberfest, have their origins here. The state is also an economic powerhouse, particularly in the automotive, technology, and finance industries, with corporations like BMW and Audi headquartered there.

A Brief History of the Region

Bavaria's history is rich and diverse, dating back to the early medieval period. It was founded as a duchy in the sixth century, and by the 12th century, it had evolved into one of the Holy Roman Empire's most powerful areas. Over the years, Bavaria played an important role in European history, particularly during the Middle Ages, and its kings frequently wielded power far beyond their borders.

After a period of political turbulence and shifting alliances in the nineteenth century, King Maximilian I Joseph established Bavaria as a monarchy in 1806. The kingdom thrived, and many of its famed castles, including the majestic Neuschwanstein Castle, were constructed during this period. However, during the Franco-Prussian War in 1871, Bavaria joined the newly unified German Empire, retaining some autonomy within it.

The twentieth century provided both struggle and change. Following World War II, Bavaria joined West Germany and eventually became one of the country's most successful and stable states. Today, it is a major actor in both Germany's cultural and economic arenas, with a strong feeling of Bavarian identity.

As I visit the region today, I notice that, while Bavaria has modernized, it has retained its traditional beauty. Its intriguing history, stunning landscapes, and rich cultural past make it a memorable destination for both visitors and residents. Whether you're wandering through Munich's lively streets, touring old castles, or relaxing in one of the many tranquil villages, Bavaria provides an experience that is profoundly connected to its history while also welcoming the future.

Why Visit Bavaria?

When I first visited Bavaria, I was charmed by the idyllic combination of breathtaking Alpine vistas, centuries-old history, and dynamic cities that appear to buzz with activity. Bavaria has a timeless quality to it while also being extremely inviting. It's a region where every nook tells a story, traditions are alive and respected, and nature's beauty is breathtaking.

The Unique Features of Bavaria
The first thing I noticed about Bavaria was its diversity. Imagine standing at the foot of the Bavarian Alps, looking up at peaks that appear to pierce the clouds, or strolling along crystal-clear

lakes like Königssee and Tegernsee. If you, like me, enjoy the great outdoors, Bavaria is a dream come true. Alpine scenery is a true gem, from hiking and skiing to simply enjoying the tranquil views.

But there's more to Bavaria than its natural beauty. The rich culture here pervades every part of existence. You'll see it in the lovely towns where inhabitants wear traditional Lederhosen and Dirndls, in the vibrant beer gardens where strangers become friends over a stein of beer, and in the festivals that liven up the streets. Let's not neglect the cities! Munich, the capital of Bavaria, is a mix of old and contemporary, with historic buildings like the Marienplatz coexisting with cutting-edge museums and trendy eateries.

Cultural and Historical Treasures
What actually distinguishes Bavaria is its strong connection to history and culture. Walking through its towns and cities is like stepping into a novel. I was blown away by the fairytale-like Neuschwanstein Castle, which inspired Disney's Sleeping Beauty Castle. Then there's Nuremberg Castle, which has stories of medieval knights and emperors.

Bavaria's history extends beyond its castles. Regensburg has well preserved Roman remains, and Würzburg's Residenz Palace dazzles with its baroque magnificence. Don't miss Bamberg, a UNESCO World Heritage site that feels like it's been preserved in time. Places like these make Bavaria feel like a living museum.

You may experience the culture here firsthand. I once attended a traditional Bavarian festival, which was filled with folk music, colorful costumes, and friendly residents. These are the moments that remind you that Bavaria is more than simply a place; it is a mood.

Natural Wonders to Explore
The natural beauty of Bavaria is, in my opinion, the cherry on top. Whether you're exploring the lush forests of the Bavarian Forest National Park or cruising the peaceful waters of Lake Chiemsee, you can't help but feel at ease and amazed. If you're looking for adventure, climbing Germany's highest peak, the Zugspitze, will leave you with unforgettable memories.

Whatever you're looking for, Bavaria has it: history, culture, adventure, or simply a place to unwind and appreciate the beauty of the globe. It's no surprise that every time I leave, I'm already arranging my next trip. Trust me—once you visit Bavaria, it will stay in your heart forever.

Best Time to Visit Bavaria

Bavaria is lovely all year round, but each season has its own distinct attraction. The greatest time to visit depends on the type of experience you want. Whether you're an enthusiastic skier, a fan of outdoor adventures, or a culture buff, there's an ideal time to visit this breathtaking region of Germany.

Winter: Skiing in the Bavarian Alps
If you enjoy winter activities, there is no better time to visit than winter. From December to March, the Bavarian Alps change into a skier's paradise. Garmisch-Partenkirchen, one of the most well-known ski resorts in the region, with excellent slopes for both beginners and advanced skiers. Even if skiing isn't your thing, there is plenty to do in the snow, from snowshoeing and tobogganing to simply absorbing the winter wonderland scenery.

The winter months also create a lovely ambiance in Bavarian communities, particularly around the holidays. Christmas markets in Munich,

Nuremberg, and other towns sparkle with dazzling lights, providing festive food, mulled wine, and handmade crafts—ideal for getting into the holiday spirit.

Spring: A Quiet Escape

Spring, from April to June, is a more relaxing time to explore Bavaria. The snow starts to melt, and the countryside bursts with wildflowers and lush foliage. The average temperature ranges between 5°C (41°F) and 15°C (59°F). This is a great time to go sightseeing without crowds. It's also an excellent time for trekking, as routes become more accessible after the snow melts but before the summer heat sets in. Towns like Füssen, near Neuschwanstein Castle, are quieter, allowing you to see the great sites without feeling rushed.

Summer: Hiking and Outdoor Adventures

Summer (June to September) is undoubtedly the ideal season for outdoor activities such as hiking and cycling. The weather is mild, with average temperatures ranging from 20°C (68°F) to 30°C (86°F), while higher altitudes in the Alps can be slightly cooler. Hiking in the Bavarian Alps during these months is spectacular. The trails are lined with wildflowers, and the vistas of the alpine lakes and mountain summits are simply breathtaking.

You can also enjoy cycling along the Danube River or visiting the attractive cities that surround Bavaria's lakes, such as Chiemsee und Tegernsee.

Summer is also an excellent season to visit famous castles such as Neuschwanstein and Hohenzollern Castle, as the grounds and gardens are in full bloom, making the experience even more romantic.

Autumn: A Bavarian Feast of Festivals
If you enjoy culture and events, autumn is the ideal time to explore Bavaria. The season's climax, of course, is Oktoberfest, Munich's world-famous beer festival, which begins in late September and runs through the first weekend of October. It's the ultimate opportunity to experience Bavarian traditions, with thousands of locals and visitors dressed in lederhosen and dirndls, eating beers, pretzels, and hearty meals while dancing and singing in large beer tents.

Even outside of Oktoberfest, autumn in Bavaria (September to November) is a magical season. The cool air, fall foliage, and harvest season make it ideal for vineyard excursions and Bavarian cuisine at intimate eateries. Fall festivities, such as Munich's Tollwood Winter Festival, are also excellent opportunities to immerse oneself in local arts and culture.

Weather Patterns Throughout The Year
Bavaria's weather is typically continental, with cold winters and pleasant summers, though it varies slightly depending on whether you're in the Alps or in a metropolis like Munich. Winters can be cold, with temperatures frequently dropping below freezing, particularly in mountainous locations, so plan for snow if you visit during these months. Summer temperatures, on the other hand, are generally nice and warm; nevertheless, infrequent rain showers might occur, particularly in the Alps, so taking a rain jacket is usually a good idea.

Spring and fall have cooler temperatures, making them ideal for touring and outdoor activities. However, because these seasons can be unpredictable, it's wise to pack layers and be ready for unexpected weather changes.

Getting to Bavaria

When it comes to going to Bavaria, you have several alternatives to make your trip as comfortable and pleasurable as possible. Having been there personally, I can confidently offer a few pointers to help you determine whether flying, driving, or taking the train is the best option for your vacation.

Flying to Bavaria

Flying is frequently the most convenient method to get to Bavaria, especially if you're traveling from abroad or a remote section of Europe. Munich Airport (MUC), one of Europe's busiest and most well-connected airports, serves as the region's principal gateway. Located around 30 kilometers (18 miles) northeast of Munich, it is contemporary, efficient, and provides easy access to other Bavarian cities via trains, buses, and car rentals.

If you're traveling to northern Bavaria, consider flying into Nuremberg Airport (NUE). It's smaller, but similarly well-organized, and ideal for seeing Franconia's old towns such as Bamberg and Würzburg. Memmingen Airport (FMM), also known as "Munich West," is another alternative for people traveling to the Bavarian Alps, particularly if flying on a budget airline.

Travel Tip: When buying flights, look for airlines that fly direct to Munich or Nuremberg. Also, I recommend downloading the airport's app for up-to-date flight information and terminal maps—it saved me a lot of time traversing Munich's massive terminals!

Driving to Bavaria

If you enjoy gorgeous road excursions (like me), driving to Bavaria can be a real treat. Bavaria is strongly connected to neighboring nations such as Austria, Switzerland, and the Czech Republic because of its massive Autobahn system. Whether you're crossing borders or beginning your journey somewhere in Germany, the drive into Bavaria is a visual feast, with rolling hills, lovely villages, and stunning Alpine views.

If you've never driven on Germany's Autobahn, here's a heads-up: certain portions have no speed limit, but others have, particularly near cities and construction zones. If you plan to cross into Austria or Switzerland, make sure your car has a valid toll sticker (vignette).

Travel Tip: Parking in major cities such as Munich can be difficult and costly. To avoid the bother, look for Park & Ride facilities on the outskirts and use public transportation to the city center.

Traveling By Train

Taking the train to Bavaria is, in my opinion, one of the most relaxing and scenic ways to travel. Germany's rail network is world-class, with high-speed trains like the ICE (InterCity Express) connecting key cities such as Munich, Nuremberg, and Regensburg. If you are traveling from another European country, direct connections are available from places such as Vienna, Zurich, and Prague.

Once in Bavaria, regional trains make it easier to get to smaller cities and villages. I recommend getting a Bayern-Ticket, a low-cost day pass that allows you to travel on regional trains, buses, and trams across Bavaria. It's ideal for seeing several sites without breaking the bank.

Travel Tip: Always double-check train schedules using the Deutsche Bahn app. Delays are rare, but they do occur, and the app is ideal for real-time updates. Furthermore, it provides mobile tickets, eliminating the need for paper copies.

Major Transportation Hubs in Bavaria
Bavaria's major transportation hubs are well-equipped to accommodate visitors arriving by air, road, or rail.

Munich Hauptbahnhof (Central Station)

Is a thriving hub for domestic and international train travel, with connections to the Munich S-Bahn and U-Bahn networks.

Nuremberg Hauptbahnhof
This smaller but equally efficient station serves northern Bavaria and connects to cities throughout Germany and Europe.

Munich ZOB (Central Bus Station)
If you arrive by coach, this new terminal provides easy access to Munich's public transportation system.

Language & Communication

When traveling around Bavaria, I quickly discovered how important language is for connecting with locals and actually understanding the region's culture. While German is the official language in Bavaria, you'll also hear the Bavarian dialect, which adds a fascinating touch to regular discussions. Don't worry—it's simple to learn a few phrases to assist you manage your trip and win the hearts of the locals.

Basic Phrases in Bavarian and German

To begin, I learnt a combination of normal German and some Bavarian phrases. While most people in towns like Munich speak German (and many also speak English), utilizing a little Bavarian can be a terrific conversation starter. Here are a few phrases I found useful:

In standard German

- Guten Tag! - Good day.

- Bitte - Please.

- Danke – Thank you.

- Entschuldigung (excuse me / sorry)

- Do you speak English? - Can you speak English?

- How much does this cost? - How much does it cost?

- Where is...? - Where is ...?

In Bavarian Dialect

- Grüß Gott! - A popular Bavarian greeting that means "God bless you" (used instead of "hello").

• Pfiat Di! - Goodbye (literally, "May God Protect You").

• Oi guade! - Best wishes!

• Minga is the Bavarian word for Munich.

• Please have a Mass Bier! - One liter of beer, please (you'll need it for Oktoberfest!).

You don't have to know every word, but using a few Bavarian phrases demonstrates respect for the local culture and generally results in a big smile.

Tips to Navigate Language Differences
While most younger Bavarians I encountered spoke good English, I noted that outside of major cities like Munich or Nuremberg, English was less often spoken. This is where my planning really paid off. Here is what I learned:

Carry a Phrasebook or Translation App
I kept a translation software like Google Translate nearby for instant assistance with signs, menus, and discussions. Offline mode proved particularly handy in rural places where Wi-Fi was not always available.

Practice Key words before your Trip
Before traveling in Bavaria, I practiced some basic German terms. Even learning how to greet someone, ask for directions, and say "thank you" boosted my confidence.

Speak Slowly and Clearly
I discovered that if I spoke slowly and clearly in English, locals were more likely to understand or make an effort to communicate. Politeness and a smile can go a long way.

Do not be Afraid to Point
When words failed me, gestures sufficed. Pointing to maps, images, or things was a simple but efficient approach to express myself.

Learn Context-specific words
For example, if you're going to a beer garden, acquiring words like Bier (beer) and Brezn (pretzel) will be quite useful. Similarly, recognizing train or bus phrases such as Bahnhof (train station) and Fahrkarte (ticket) is beneficial for navigating.

Enjoy the Experience
Even when I made blunders while trying to speak their language, the people were always friendly and

patient. It became part of the enjoyment, and I felt more connected to the folks I met.

Chapter 2: Planning Your Trip to Bavaria

Budgeting and Cost of Travel

Setting a realistic budget while planning your trip to Bavaria can help you have a stress-free and pleasurable experience. Having recently gone through this wonderful location, I'd like to discuss what you may expect in terms of expenses and how to make the most of your trip without breaking the bank.

Estimated Travel Expenses

Accommodation Costs
Bavaria has a wide variety of hotel alternatives to suit all budgets. For a mid-range visitor, hotels in Munich or Nuremberg normally cost between €100 and €150 per night for a double room. Hostels or guesthouses are excellent options for budget tourists, with nightly rates ranging from €30 to €60. If you desire a more unique experience, consider renting a room in a Bavarian Gasthof (traditional inn) in the countryside for roughly €70-€100 per night.

Meals and Dining
Bavarian cuisine is not only good, but also quite inexpensive. A supper at a local beer garden or traditional tavern costs between €10 and €15, and includes robust foods such as schnitzel, sausages, and pretzels. For a more upmarket dining experience, budget between €30 and €50 per person. Breakfast is frequently included in hotel stays, and street sellers or markets offer quick eats for less than €5-€7.

Transportation Costs
Bavaria boasts a great public transportation system. A day pass for regional trains (Bayern-Ticket) costs roughly €27-€32 and provides unrestricted travel for one person, with savings possible for group

travel. Renting a car to explore the Bavarian Alps or distant places costs between €40 and €60 per day, excluding gasoline.

Attractions & Activities
The majority of attractions have extremely reasonable entry fees. Visiting prominent landmarks such as Neuschwanstein Castle costs approximately €15 per adult, while many museums charge between €5 and €12. Don't forget that many outdoor activities, such as hiking or seeing picturesque lakes, are free!

Tips to Save Money While Visiting Bavaria

Use public Transportation
Instead of renting a car, take use of Bavaria's efficient rail and bus networks. The Bayern-Ticket is especially beneficial, as it allows for unlimited travel on regional trains and buses across Bavaria for the full day. It's a great deal if you're touring several cities or towns in one day.

Plan Around Seasonal Deals
If you are flexible about your trip dates, coming during the shoulder seasons (spring and fall) can save you money on both lodging and flights.

Furthermore, these periods are less crowded, providing a more real experience.

Dine Like A Local
Instead of costly tourist meals, try beer gardens or local bars. You'll get a great deal and enjoy real Bavarian cuisine. Markets such as Viktualienmarkt in Munich are also ideal for purchasing fresh, inexpensive snacks or meals.

Take Advantage of Free Activities
Bavaria is rich in free or low-cost activities. Enjoy the spectacular architecture of Munich's Marienplatz, trek through the Bavarian Alps, or relax by lakes such as Tegernsee or Königssee for free. Many towns provide free walking tours; remember to tip the guide!

Stay in Small Towns
Accommodations in Munich and major cities can be expensive, especially around Oktoberfest. Consider staying in nearby smaller cities like Augsburg or Regensburg, where rates are lower and you can still easily access main attractions by train.

Accommodation Options

Everyone can find a place to stay in Bavaria. Whether you want to splurge on a luxury hotel, stick to a budget-friendly hostel, or do something genuinely unusual like stay in a castle or an alpine cabin, Bavaria has it all. Let me walk you through some of the better solutions I've discovered.

Best Hotels, Hostels, and Airbnb Options for Every Budget

One of my favourite aspects of Bavaria is the variety of accommodation alternatives available to suit a wide range of budgets and preferences.

Luxury Hotels

If you want to treat yourself, towns like Munich and Nuremberg have plenty of high-end hotels to choose from. The Hotel Bayerischer Hof in Munich is a classic, combining modern conveniences with old-world charm. For something as amazing but a little more relaxed, the Schloss Elmau, located in the Alps, provides a tranquil getaway equipped with a spa and breathtaking mountain views.

Mid-Range Options

For guests seeking comfort without breaking the budget, Bavaria has some outstanding mid-range hotels. The H4 Hotel Residenzschloss in Bayreuth is a personal favorite, with its perfect blend of historical charm and modern comfort. Meanwhile, in Regensburg, the Sorat Insel-Hotel is located right on the Danube River, providing magnificent views and convenient access to the city's UNESCO World Heritage monuments.

Budget-Friendly Stays
If you're traveling on a tight budget, don't worry—Bavaria boasts plenty of hostels and low-cost hotels that don't sacrifice quality. I've stayed at Wombat's City Hostel in Munich, and it's usually bustling with a lively, multinational atmosphere. Another excellent alternative is the Jugendherberge Berchtesgaden (Berchtesgaden Youth Hostel), which is ideal for visiting the surrounding Alpes.

Airbnb
Airbnb is an excellent choice for a more personalized experience in Bavaria. From sophisticated Munich apartments to comfortable farm stays in rural locations, there is something for everyone, regardless of style or budget. One notable Airbnb is a rural farmhouse near Garmisch-Partenkirchen, where you can wake up to

the sound of cowbells and enjoy breathtaking mountain views.

Unique Stays: Castles, Alpine Cabins, and Countryside Hotels

If you're seeking for something genuinely unusual, Bavaria's hotel alternatives will astound you.

Stay at a Castle

Have you ever wanted to live like royalty? Bavaria is home to various castles that are now used as hotels. Schloss Neuschwanstein does not offer overnight accommodations, however the nearby Hotel Müller Hohenschwangau offers breathtaking views of this historic monument. For a true castle experience, I recommend Burg Colmberg, a medieval fortification that has been turned into a hotel. There's nothing quite like waking up in a castle surrounded by hills and ancient stone walls.

Alpine Cabins

If you're visiting the Bavarian Alps, consider staying in a quaint mountain cabin. These rustic retreats are ideal for people looking to disconnect and immerse themselves in nature. I slept in a chalet near Lake Tegernsee, where the mornings were filled with fresh mountain air and stunning vistas, while the nights were spent under a blanket of stars.

Countryside Hotels

For those seeking a gentler pace, Bavaria's countryside hotels provide a tranquil respite. Many of these are family-owned businesses that will treat you like one of their own. One of my favorite hotels is the Landhotel Huberhof near Chiemsee; it's a wonderful establishment with a friendly, welcoming environment and convenient access to outdoor sports.

Transportation Within Bavaria

When I first arrived in Bavaria, I was pleasantly pleased by how easy it is to move around, whether you're in the bustling metropolis of Munich, the lovely streets of Nuremberg, or exploring the breathtaking Bavarian Alps. Here's what I discovered about the various transit alternatives accessible in the region.

Getting Around Munich, Nuremberg, and Other Cities

Bavaria's cities are well-connected, and navigating them is simple, even for those unfamiliar with the area. Munich has one of the most efficient public transit systems I've ever used. The U-Bahn (subway), S-Bahn (commuter trains), trams, and buses make it quite convenient to get around. If you're staying in the city center, the Munich City Pass is worth considering because it provides unrestricted access to all public transportation and discounts on numerous attractions.

Nuremberg's transportation system is equally convenient, with a well-organized network of trams and buses. The Nuremberg Card provides similar perks, including access to public transit and free or reduced admission to popular museums and sites.

Even smaller cities, such as Regensburg and Augsburg, have reliable public transportation. Most of these cities also have bike-sharing programs, which I found to be an enjoyable way to explore at my own pace.

Public Transportation, Car Rentals, and Bicycle Tours
Bavaria offers an excellent range of public transportation alternatives. I utilized the Bavarian Regional Ticket (Bayernticket), which was ideal for a day trip outside of the larger cities. This pass allows you to travel on regional trains, buses, and trams throughout Bavaria for a very low cost, making it ideal for day visits to locations like Neuschwanstein Castle or Garmisch-Partenkirchen.

When I wanted to visit the Bavarian countryside or travel between cities, I chose vehicle rentals. While public transportation is quite efficient, having the option to rent a car allowed me more flexibility, particularly for isolated locations or last-minute adjustments to my plan. Driving through picturesque roads and farmland was one of the pleasures of my trip. The roads are well-kept, and parking is generally accessible at most tourist attractions. Just be sure you understand the Autobahn restrictions if you intend to travel far!

If you enjoy cycling as I do, Bavaria has some wonderful bike excursions. Munich, for example, is a bike-friendly city with many bike lanes to explore, including routes through Englischer Garten, one of the world's largest urban parks. There are numerous guided bike tours available, particularly in Munich and Nuremberg, which allow you to learn about the city's history and culture while pedaling around its streets.

Explore the Bavarian Alps and Rural Villages
I recommend renting a car to fully experience the Bavarian Alps' splendor. The train can transport you to larger towns like Garmisch-Partenkirchen or

Berchtesgaden, but a car provides the most flexibility for getting to more rural communities or going on alpine adventures.

However, if you are not comfortable driving, bus tours to the Bavarian Alps are available, and they include access to hiking trails, lakes, and attractive villages such as Mittenwald. Ski shuttles are commonly used to transport visitors from large cities to ski slopes during the winter season.

Bavaria is a hiking enthusiast's heaven. While certain trails are easily accessible by public transportation, private mountain taxis can take you to higher altitudes if you prefer a shorter route. Don't forget that you may rent bikes, including electric cycles, to explore the rural communities and surrounding hills. The Romantic Road is a popular cycling tour route that passes through lovely towns such as Dinkelsbühl und Rothenburg ob der Tauber.

Safety Tips and Emergency Information

When traveling in Bavaria, it is critical to keep educated and prepared for any unexpected circumstances. While the location is generally extremely safe, knowing the local emergency contacts, healthcare choices, and safety requirements will help you feel more at ease throughout your vacation.

Local Emergency Contacts

In an emergency, you can contact the following services:

Emergency number (police, fire, ambulance): 112

This is Germany's general emergency number for police, fire, and medical situations. You can call this number free from any phone, and the operators speak English.

Police: 110

Dial 110 for any police-related emergencies. If you are engaged in a traffic incident, have your information available when speaking with officials.

Local Hospitals and Clinics

- **Munich:** Klinikum rechts der Isar (Hospital) - +49 89 4140

- **Nuremberg:** St. Theresien Hospital, +49 911 6303 0

- **Other Regions:** Most cities have local hospitals, and pharmacies can help with minor ailments or medicine needs. A green cross indicates a pharmacy.

Pharmacy (Apotheke)
Many pharmacies in Bavaria stay open late, with a 24-hour emergency pharmacy in each large city. You may quickly find the nearest pharmacy by looking for a sign that says "Apotheke" or by using the "ADAC" app, which helps you discover pharmacies in crises.

Healthcare in Bavaria
Bavaria boasts an outstanding healthcare system. If you need medical care, you can easily visit a hospital or a local clinic, and pharmacies can be found in practically every town or village.

EU Citizens
If you have an EHIC (European Health Insurance Card), you can receive emergency care in Germany at no cost. Non-EU citizens, on the other hand, should seriously consider purchasing travel insurance that includes healthcare coverage.

Non-EU Citizens

Medical treatment is best provided by travel insurance that covers medical expenses, as healthcare costs might be prohibitively expensive without it. Ensure that your coverage covers both emergency and non-emergency medical circumstances.

Safety Guidelines
Bavaria is one of the safest locations in Europe, however there are a few precautions you should take to have a worry-free trip:

Keep your Belongings Safe
While minor crime is uncommon, like with any tourist area, it's wise to keep your belongings safe. Passports, credit cards, and substantial sums of cash should be carried in a money belt or hidden bag.

Public Transportation
Public transit in Bavaria is dependable and secure. However, use caution with your valuables, especially during peak hours in train stations and subways.

Outdoor Activities
If you want to trek in the Alps or visit remote locations, make sure you have the necessary

equipment, stick to established trails, and notify someone of your plans in case of an emergency.

Weather Precautions
Bavaria's weather can be unpredictable, particularly in the highlands. Check the weather forecast before going outside. Winter roads can be treacherous, so exercise caution when driving, especially in rural regions.

Travel Insurance and Essential Preparations
Before heading to Bavaria, I strongly advise you to obtain travel insurance to protect yourself from unforeseen occurrences. Travel insurance can cover the following:

- Trip cancellation or interruption

- Lost or stolen luggage.

- Medical emergencies.

- Flight delays and cancellations

Having this peace of mind means you won't have to worry about unforeseen expenses. Most travel insurance providers provide extensive coverage that meets a variety of demands, so select the one that best suits your travel style.

In addition, create a backup plan in case of an emergency. It's a good idea to keep the contact information for your embassy or consulate available, especially if you're coming from outside the EU. Knowing where the nearest hospital is, knowing basic German words for emergencies, and understanding how the healthcare system works can all save time in emergency situations.

Cultural Etiquette and Local Customs

When I first arrived in Bavaria, I was impressed by how friendly and warm the locals were. Bavarians are proud of their traditions, and understanding them might enhance your experience. Whether you're having a beer in Munich's famous beer gardens or seeing the lovely villages of the Bavarian Alps, knowing a little about local etiquette might help you make a positive impression.

Bavarian Customs and Manners
Respect and courtesy are highly valued in Bavarian culture. While many people speak English, particularly in cities, knowing a few German phrases can make a significant difference. A simple

"Guten Tag" (Good day) or "Grüß Gott" (Hello, literally "God greets you") is usually welcomed with a smile and may even start a conversation. In rural areas, Bavarians frequently prefer more formal titles like "Herr" (Mr.) or "Frau" (Mrs.), thus when in doubt, err on the side of formality.

Bavarians are proud of their ancestry, and it is usual to see people dressed in traditional clothes, particularly during festivals. If you're lucky enough to be invited to a traditional event like Oktoberfest, you might notice locals dressed in dirndls and lederhosen. While you are not required to wear these costumes, showing respect for local customs and traditions is always welcomed.

Tips and Dining Etiquette
Tipping is an essential aspect of Bavarian culture, however more modest than in other nations such as the United States. In restaurants, it is common to tip between 5-10% of the bill, depending on the level of service. If you're dining in a more casual atmosphere, rounding up the cost is usually sufficient. For example, if your dinner costs €22, leaving €25 is completely acceptable. Money's also typical to tip the waitress directly rather than leaving money on the table.

In cafés or casual restaurants, if you order at the counter and then take a seat, you may not need to tip as much. However, if you are seated and served at the table, a gratuity of €1-2 is appropriate for smaller meals.

Bavarians love long, unhurried dinners, frequently accompanied by beer or wine. If you are asked to go to someone's home for dinner, it is customary to bring a little gift, such as a bottle of wine or flowers. It is also customary for visitors to make a toast before the meal begins, with the typical Bavarian toast being "Prost!"" (Thank you!).

When dining in restaurants or cafés, it is critical to maintain proper table manners. Keep your hands on the table, but not your elbows. Don't begin eating until everyone at the table has been served, and it's polite to wait for the host to start the meal first. If you're at a large party, you may hear the word "Mahlzeit" (dinner time), which is used to greet everyone and wish them a good dinner.

Local Greetings
Greetings are very important to Bavarians. When meeting someone, a forceful handshake is usual, especially in business situations. A kiss on both cheeks is a typical welcome for friends and family,

though this varies by location. In more rural places, people may be more reserved until they get to know you, so always approach politely and with an open mind.

In addition to "Grüß Gott," another popular greeting in Bavaria is "Servus," which can be used to signify both hello and goodbye. It is a warm, informal greeting, therefore feel free to use it in casual contexts. If you're in Munich, you'll frequently hear "O'zapft ist!" (It's tapped!) is a well-known phrase shouted at the start of Oktoberfest to signify the tapping of the first barrel of beer.

Bavarians cherish their time, thus timeliness is essential. If you have a meeting or dinner invitation, make sure to appear on time. Arriving late may be perceived as impolite or insensitive.

Chapter 3: Must-See Destinations in Bavaria

Munich The Heart of Bavaria

When I first arrived in Munich, I was struck by the city's distinct blend of history, culture, and modern energy. This city truly reflects the spirit of Bavaria, with something for everyone, whether you're a history buff, a foodie, or just trying to soak up the local culture.

Must-See Sites in Munich

Marienplatz

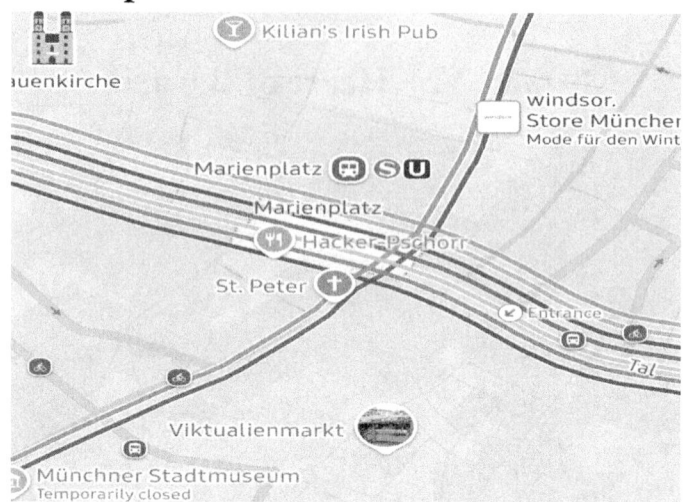

Marienplatz, Munich's lively center square, is located in the heart of the city. Standing here, you can't miss the breathtaking Neues Rathaus (New Town Hall), which features exquisite Gothic architecture and the iconic Glockenspiel clock tower. Every day, thousands visit to watch its adorable characters reenact Bavarian legends, a spectacle that never disappoints. Marienplatz is the city's living room, with a vibrant Christmas market in December and open-air concerts in the summer. It's a must-see no matter what season.

Nymphenburg Palace

I urge that you visit the majestic Nymphenburg Palace to learn about Bavaria's royal history. This huge Baroque masterpiece was originally the summer home of Bavarian rulers, and it's just as grand as you'd expect. Walking through its sumptuous rooms, from the fresco-adorned Great Hall to the Rococo-styled Amalienburg hunting lodge, is like entering into a fairytale. Don't miss the gardens, which are ideal for a leisurely stroll and feature fountains, sculptures, and calm canals.

English Garden

If you want to take a break from sightseeing, visit the English Garden, one of the world's largest urban parks. It is more than just a park; it is a way of life in Munich. The Chinesischer Turm (Chinese Tower) beer garden attracts locals who want to sunbathe, exercise, or enjoy a refreshing drink. Personally, I enjoyed watching surfers ride the waves on the Eisbach, the park's one-of-a-kind man-made river. It's an ideal place to relax and experience the Bavarian way of life.

Beer Gardens, Historical Sites, and Contemporary Attractions

Beer Gardens

Speaking of beer, you can't visit Munich without visiting its famous beer gardens. One of my faves was the Hofbräuhaus, a classic beer hall that still exudes Bavarian Gemütlichkeit (coziness). Whether you're drinking a Maß (a liter of beer) or eating traditional meals like pretzels and Weißwurst, the atmosphere is unparalleled. The Augustiner-Keller beer garden is a more casual outdoor option that locals enjoy.

Historic Sites

Munich's history is both fascinating and difficult. There's a lot to see, from the stately Residenz palace, which depicts the past of Bavarian nobility, to the gloomy Dachau Memorial just outside the city. Walking around the Viktualienmarkt, a famous open-air market, I felt a connection to Munich's centuries-long legacy of local business.

Modern Attractions

While Munich honors its history, it is also strongly entrenched in the present. The futuristic BMW Welt exemplifies German engineering at its finest, while the Olympic Park, built for the 1972 games, continues to serve as a concert and event venue. For art enthusiasts, the Pinakothek museums house everything from Renaissance masterpieces to cutting-edge contemporary art.

Neuschwanstein Castle

Neuschwanstein Castle is the one spot in Bavaria that actually feels like you've stepped into a fairytale. This majestic castle, located on a mountaintop above the village of Hohenschwangau near Füssen, is one of Germany's most well-known monuments. It's a site where dreams come true, thanks to its soaring turrets, scenic setting, and extensive history.

A Glimpse into History

King Ludwig II of Bavaria, also known as the "Fairy Tale King," commissioned Neuschwanstein Castle in the nineteenth century. Ludwig, who rose to the throne at the age of 18, was fascinated by historical castles and Wagnerian operas, and he planned Neuschwanstein as a monument to the great composer Richard Wagner. Though the castle was never finished (Ludwig died abruptly in 1886), it is nevertheless an awe-inspiring emblem of his unique vision.

The architecture is a stunning blend of romanticism and medieval style, with ornate interiors and towers that appear to touch the sky. The castle was built as a private getaway for Ludwig, but after his death, it was accessible to the public. Today, millions of visitors come each year to admire its magnificence, but like with any major tourist spot, there are methods to make your stay more enjoyable.

Touring the Castle
The castle itself provides a variety of guided tours that take visitors through the most renowned chambers, including the throne hall, King Ludwig's bedroom, and the spectacular dining room. The tours are well-organized, and while the interior of the castle is small in comparison to other big European castles, it remains a remarkable

experience. The stories surrounding the castle's construction, Ludwig's life, and his unexplained death offer an intriguing dimension to your visit.

When visiting, don't miss the Marienbrücke Bridge, which provides the greatest views of the castle framed by the surrounding mountains and forests. The environment surrounding Neuschwanstein is as attractive as the castle itself, with the adjoining Alpsee Lake and Hohenschwangau Castle providing extra photo opportunities and historical context.

Best ways to get there and Avoid Crowds
Neuschwanstein Castle is accessible by automobile, but you must park in the village of Hohenschwangau and then walk, take a bus, or ride a horse-drawn carriage up the hill. The trek to the castle is attractive and relatively short, but it can be congested, particularly during the summer months. To avoid crowds, I recommend arriving early in the morning, when the castle first opens, or later in the afternoon, after most tourists have left.

The castle is also accessible by train from Munich, with a picturesque route that takes you near Füssen, followed by a short bus ride to the entrance. If you're staying in Munich, try arranging a guided day trip, which frequently includes transportation and skip-the-line admission, allowing you to escape the long lines that sometimes occur during peak seasons.

For those who prefer a more peaceful experience, going during the off-season (late fall or early spring) is ideal. Lines are shorter, and you'll have more time to explore the surrounding region without the throng.

The Bavarian Alps

When I think about the Bavarian Alps, I am taken to a region of breathtaking natural beauty, where adventure and tranquility coexist. One of my favorite places in this spectacular mountain range is Garmisch-Partenkirchen, a picturesque hamlet perched at the foot of Zugspitze, Germany's highest point. Whether you visit in the winter or summer, this location has something for everyone.

Skiing at Garmisch-Partenkirchen and Zugspitze

If you enjoy winter sports, Garmisch-Partenkirchen is a dream come true. The ski resort is well-known for its diverse slopes that appeal to skiers of all skill levels, from novices to seasoned professionals. I've had the opportunity to ski down the slopes of Zugspitze, where the vista from the summit is nothing short of spectacular—snow-capped peaks spanning as far as the eye can see. It is hardly surprising that Garmisch-Partenkirchen has hosted World Cup skiing events. After a day on the slopes, I recommend stopping by one of the comfortable alpine huts for a cup of mulled wine or a hearty bowl of potato soup to warm up.

Even if skiing isn't your thing, Zugspitze is nevertheless worth visiting all year. On clear days, I rode the cable car to the summit and enjoyed the panoramic views over Germany, Austria, and even Switzerland. There's something special about being at the top of the Alps, knowing you've reached Germany's highest point.

Hiking & Adventure Sports
When the snow melts and the flowers blossom, Garmisch-Partenkirchen transforms into a hiking paradise. I've spent hours hiking the countless trails, which range from moderate, family-friendly tracks to more difficult treks that take you deep into the mountains. The Partnach valley is a route I'll never forget. I strolled alongside the thunderous waterfall, the cool mist from the river cooling my face as I followed the winding path into the rocky valley. It's one of those places that makes you feel little in the greatest manner possible, with nature's magnificence on display.

For the more daring, the Bavarian Alps offer rock climbing, paragliding, and mountain riding. On my last visit, I joined a group for a paragliding trip over Garmisch-Partenkirchen, and it was absolutely amazing to glide over the alpine meadows and lakes below, surrounded by hills on all sides.

Mountain Villages and Scenic Drives
One of my favorite things about the Bavarian Alps is the tranquil mountain communities that dot the landscape. These small villages provide a look into

traditional Bavarian living, with inhabitants gathering in beer gardens to tell stories and enjoy a slower pace of life. I spent the day exploring the village of Oberammergau, which is known for its wood carvings and lovely buildings with frescoed walls. Walking through the cobblestone streets, I felt as if I had slipped into a novel.

The picturesque drives through the Bavarian Alps are among the nicest I've ever experienced. The Alpine Road, also known as the "Deutsche Alpenstraße," should not be missed. This road passes through some of Germany's most beautiful mountain vistas, passing lush woods, alpine meadows, and tranquil lakes. I took my time, pausing along the route to admire the scenery, take photos, and enjoy a quiet moment by the lake.

Nuremberg Medieval Charm

When I initially arrived in Nuremberg, I felt like I had gone back in time. This city, with its well maintained medieval beauty and layers of history, provides a beautiful yet humbling experience. Walking through the cobblestone lanes of the Old Town, you'll be surrounded by half-timbered buildings, Gothic churches, and a diverse range of historical and cultural sites.

Exploring Nuremberg's Icons

One of my first stops was the impressive Nuremberg Castle, which has served as a symbol of the city's importance since the Middle Ages.

Climbing to the top of the castle grounds provided me with spectacular panoramic views of the city, which wonderfully captured Nuremberg's medieval architecture. Don't miss the Sinwell Tower, which provides insight into the castle's past and showcases its defensive architecture.

From there, I wandered down to the Old Town (Altstadt), a vibrant and charming neighborhood. The charming Weißgerbergasse is a street dotted with classic artisan buildings that showcases Nuremberg's craftsmanship heritage. Some of my favorite sites in the Old Town are the bustling Hauptmarkt square. If you go during the holidays, you'll be treated to the world-famous Christkindlesmarkt (Christmas Market). Trust me, this market is a sensory feast—with the aroma of roasted almonds, the dazzle of holiday lights, and the seductive warmth of mulled wine.

City's WWII History and Monuments
While Nuremberg is deeply rooted in its medieval past, it also played a pivotal role in more recent history, particularly during World War II. As I explored, I couldn't help but think about the city's transformation from a center of Nazi propaganda to a beacon of accountability through the Nuremberg Trials.

The Documentation Center Nazi Party Rally Grounds is a must-see for everyone interested in understanding this complicated period of history. Walking through the gloomy, unfinished Congress Hall and standing in the massive Zeppelinfeld arena, I was struck by the size of the propaganda machine. The museum's interactive exhibits offer compelling insights into the development and demise of the Nazi regime.

Later, I went to Courtroom 600 at the Palace of Justice, where the Nuremberg Trials took place. Standing in the room where justice was given following one of humanity's worst eras was both emotional and thought-provoking. The companion exhibition explores the legal and historical significance of the trials, a watershed moment in history that continues to affect international law today.

Why Nuremberg Fascinates Me
What distinguishes Nuremberg is its ability to mix medieval charm with historical significance. It's a city that begs you to admire its beauty while thinking about its history. Whether you're climbing the castle walls, enjoying the Christmas Market, or

learning about WWII, Nuremberg provides an incredible journey through time.

Regensburg & Bamberg

As I journeyed through Bavaria, I became charmed by Regensburg and Bamberg, two lovely medieval cities that appear trapped in time while nevertheless alive with history and culture. These villages, with their lovely cobblestone alleys, well-preserved architecture, and picturesque riverfront views, feel like entering into a fairy tale.

Regensburg

59

Regensburg, a UNESCO World Heritage Site, is one of Germany's best preserved medieval towns. The combination of Roman, Gothic, and medieval inspirations captivated me. The city's Old Town is a tangle of narrow streets and picturesque squares, with a piece of history hidden around each corner. Walking along the famed Stone Bridge (Steinerne Brücke), which dates back to the 12th century, I marveled at the views of the Danube River and the city skyline, which was peppered with church spires.

One of my first trips was at Regensburg Cathedral (Dom St. Peter), an important specimen of Gothic architecture. Its lofty spires and beautiful stained glass windows astounded me. As I went through town, I came across charming cafés, each with a stunning view of the river, where I stopped to drink a coffee and soak up the tranquil atmosphere. The Historical Sausage Kitchen (Historische Wurstküche), one of Germany's oldest eateries, prepared a plate of Regensburg's famous sausages that was simply amazing.

Regensburg also houses the Thurn und Taxis Palace, a grandiose baroque edifice with stunning grounds. A walk through the palace grounds was an excellent way to experience the splendor of the past, and the views over the city from here were breathtaking.

Bamberg

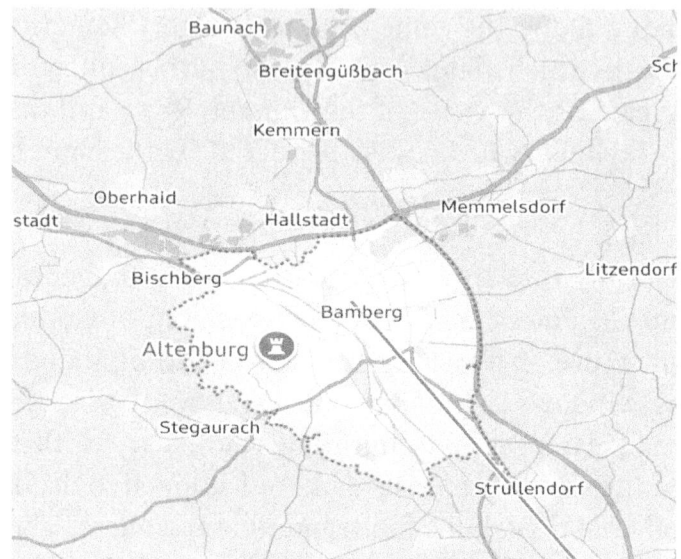

A short drive away, Bamberg provides a slightly quieter yet equally captivating experience. This town, set on seven hills, has a distinct beauty, with historic homes and cobbled lanes lining the banks of the Regnitz River. As I explored the ancient town, I felt transported to another time, particularly around the Bamberg Cathedral, which dominates the skyline with its twin towers.

One of the city's most photographed landmarks is the Old Town Hall (Altes Rathaus), which is located on a bridge in the middle of the river. As I stood on the bridge, gazing at the colorful edifice covered with paintings, I couldn't help but love the picturesque surroundings.

One of the joys of my trip to Bamberg was the beer culture. The city's local breweries serve Rauchbier, a unique brew with a rich, smoky flavor that I couldn't resist drinking at a quaint neighborhood tavern. The Bamberger Beer Trail led me to numerous ancient breweries, where I learnt about the centuries-old brewing traditions that still exist in this little city.

Both towns provide Riverside Views
What I liked best about Regensburg and Bamberg were the tranquil riverfront views that each town provided. Whether I was wandering along the banks of the Danube in Regensburg or enjoying the tranquil waters of the Regnitz in Bamberg, I discovered a sense of tranquility that was difficult to match. These towns are ideal for anyone who wants to get away from the hustle and bustle of larger cities while still enjoying Bavaria's rich history and culture.

Visiting Regensburg and Bamberg seemed like going back in time, but both towns are so vibrant with culture, delicious food, and genuine Bavarian friendliness that I left with a sense of nostalgia and a strong want to return. Whether you're a history buff, an admirer of medieval architecture, or simply looking for a scenic vacation, these two towns are a must-see on any trip to Bavaria.

Chapter 4: Bavarian Culture and Traditions

Oktoberfest

When I think of Bavaria, Oktoberfest quickly comes to mind. As someone who has been lucky enough to attend this world-famous event, I can assure you that it is much more than just a beer festival; it is a vibrant celebration of Bavarian culture, history, and brotherhood. Let me walk you through what makes Oktoberfest so memorable, and provide some insider ideas to make your experience unforgettable.

A Brief History of Oktoberfest

Oktoberfest originated in 1810 as a royal festivity. Crown Prince Ludwig (later King Ludwig I) married Princess Therese of Saxe-Hildburghausen, and Munich residents were invited to attend the celebrations on a vast meadow outside the city gates. The festival included horse racing, music, and food, and it was so popular that the city decided to make it an annual event. Today, the meadow—Theresienwiese—welcomes millions of guests each year for what has become the world's largest folk festival.

Oktoberfest began as an agricultural festival, but has now expanded to include amusement rides, food stalls, and, most importantly, beer tents. Despite delays caused by wars and pandemics, the celebration has endured, embodying the best of Bavarian culture.

Events and What to Expect

Arriving at Oktoberfest feels like entering another universe. Imagine a gigantic fairground filled with colorful tents, lively beer gardens, thrilling amusement rides, and the delightful smells of Bavarian cuisine. Here's what to expect:

Opening Day Parade

The event begins with the grand entrance of the Wiesn landlords and breweries, followed by a traditional costume and riflemen's procession. It's a visual feast and an excellent opportunity to witness true Bavarian clothing in its full glory.

The Beer Tents
There are 14 huge beer tents and 20 smaller ones, each with its own unique atmosphere. Personal favorites include the classic Hofbräu, Augustiner, and Schottenhamel tents. Make sure to drink a Maß (one-liter beer) made specifically for Oktoberfest by Munich's leading breweries.

Traditional Food
Pair your beer with robust Bavarian fare such as roast chicken (Hendl), pig knuckles (Schweinshaxe), and gigantic pretzel. Both the beer and the meal are highlights!

Live Music and Dance
Every tent has traditional brass bands playing Bavarian folk tunes, pop songs, and drinking anthems. Don't be shy: join the people in singing and dancing on the benches.

Family-friendly Days

If you're coming with children, Tuesdays at Oktoberfest are designated family days, featuring cheap rides and activities for younger guests.

Tips for Attending Oktoberfest
During my first visit to Oktoberfest, I learned a few hard lessons. Here are my best ideas to help you get the most out of your experience:

Get there Early
Tents fill up quickly, particularly on weekends. Arrive by ten a.m. to secure an excellent position.

Wear Traditional Attire
Nothing makes you feel more included in the celebration than wearing a Dirndl or Lederhosen. These are commonly available for rental or purchase in Munich prior to the festival.

Reserve a Table
If you're visiting with a group, make a reservation in advance. Otherwise, you may have trouble finding a seat during busy hours.

Bring Cash
Many vendors and beer tents accept cash only, so keep Euros handy for beer, food, and souvenirs.

Know Your Limits
A Maß is stronger than your typical beer, so plan accordingly to enjoy the entire day (or days!) of festivities. Stay hydrated and consume lots of food to keep going.

The Importance of beer Culture in Bavaria
In Bavaria, beer is more than just a beverage; it is a way of life. The region is home to some of the world's oldest breweries, many of which follow the Reinheitsgebot, the Bavarian Purity Law of 1516. This regulation requires that only water, hops, and malt be used in brewing, preserving the quality and history of Bavarian beer.

Oktoberfest celebrates the rich beer tradition like no other event. The six Munich breweries who contribute beer to the festival—Augustiner, Paulaner, Spaten, Löwenbräu, Hacker-Pschorr, and Hofbräu—create unique beers for the occasion. These beers are slightly stronger and fuller-bodied, making them ideal for a celebratory setting.

But beer culture in Bavaria is not limited to Oktoberfest. Beer gardens and halls serve as social hubs throughout the year, bringing together locals and guests to enjoy drinks, tales, and laughter. It is a pillar of Bavarian hospitality and communal spirit.

Why Oktoberfest is a Must-Try
Oktoberfest was more than a festival to me; it was an immersion into Bavarian culture. The lively atmosphere, nice people, and centuries-old traditions make for an unforgettable experience. Whether you're there for the beer, the cuisine, the music, or simply the joy of celebration, Oktoberfest is an experience that will linger long after you've left the tents.

Bavarian Cuisine

When I think of Bavarian cuisine, I can't help but feel relaxed and pleasant. The food here is more than just filling your stomach; it's about celebrating the region's rich culture and traditions. Bavarian cuisine has been developed over decades, and whether you dine at a rustic beer hall or in a Michelin-starred restaurant, the flavors will definitely leave an impact.

Traditional Bavarian Dishes To Try

Weißwurst (Bavarian white sausage)

Weißwurst, one of Bavaria's most popular meals, is an absolute must-try. These delicate white sausages, originally cooked with minced veal and hog back bacon, are lightly seasoned with parsley, lemon, mace, onions, and cardamom. They're normally served with sweet mustard and freshly baked Bretzen (pretzels), and I've discovered that there's nothing better than pairing them with a cool lager. It's an authentic Bavarian experience!

Pretzel (Bretzen)
Ah, the Bavarian pretzel: crunchy on the exterior, soft and doughy on the inside. These massive, twisted sweets may be found everywhere, from street food vendors to the most upscale eateries. The dough and its trademark golden-brown crust hold the key to making the ideal pretzel. A pretzel is an iconic symbol of Bavarian hospitality, whether it's served with a cold beer in a beer garden or as a snack between meals.

Schweinshaxe (pork Knuckle)
For those with a hearty appetite, Schweinshaxe is a Bavarian delicacy not to be missed. The soft pig knuckle is roasted to perfection, leaving the skin wonderfully crunchy. This dish, usually paired with sauerkraut or red cabbage with dumplings, represents the comfort and tradition of Bavarian

cuisine. Each bite is rich, savory, and gratifying. I've frequently found it to be the highlight of a hearty lunch eaten with friends in one of the region's beer halls.

Dumplings (knödel)
Dumplings can be found in every region of Bavaria, served with almost every meal. These pillowy treats, whether composed of bread or potatoes, pair perfectly with rich meat dishes such as roast pork or Sauerbraten (pot roast). They're incredibly filling and the ideal way to soak up the delectable sauces that accompany Bavarian dishes.

Obatzda
This creamy cheese spread is a popular snack served with toast or pretzels. It's a delicious, tangy dish made with camembert cheese, butter, onions, and a sprinkle of paprika that goes well with a cool lager. It's a beer garden favorite and an excellent introduction to Bavarian cheese culture.

Where To Eat
Bavaria is famed for its beer halls and rustic eating experiences, but it also has a fine-dining scene that rivals the best in Europe. Here are some places that I recommend:

Traditional Beer Halls

You haven't truly experienced Bavaria until you sit in a typical beer hall. The environment is lively and pleasant, with big tables and free flowing beer. Munich's Hofbräuhaus is the city's most famous beer hall, where you can eat hearty Bavarian dishes while listening to traditional music and the clink of beer steins. Another popular establishment is the Augustiner Bräu, which is well-known for its delectable sausages, substantial stews, and, of course, its own beer.

Biergarten Dining

On beautiful days, Bavarians come to the Biergarten (beer garden) to have their meals outside. Chinesischer Turm in Munich's English Garden is one of the city's most well-known beer gardens, where you can enjoy a variety of local cuisine, from sausages to pretzels, while taking in the gorgeous surroundings. Biergarten am See at Tegernsee provides a lakeside experience with pretzels and Weissbier while overlooking the mountains.

Michelin-Starred Restaurants

If you want to upgrade your Bavarian dining experience, there are several wonderful Michelin-starred restaurants that provide a modern take on classic dishes. Tantris in Munich is a world-renowned restaurant that combines traditional Bavarian cuisine with cutting-edge technology. The emphasis is on seasonal and local ingredients, resulting in dishes that are both inventive and steeped in the region's culinary traditions. Dallmayr is another Michelin-starred restaurant in Munich that provides an exceptional fine-dining experience combining Bavarian and international flavors.

Farm-to-table and Regional Dining
For a more true taste of Bavaria, seek out farm-to-table eateries that use locally sourced ingredients. Gasthof Obermüller in the Allgäu area serves traditional meals made with fresh, locally sourced produce and meats, and the environment is warm and welcoming. Small, family-run restaurants in Franconia offer excellent wine and cuisine pairings that emphasize the region's wine tradition.

Folk Traditions and Festivals

When I think about Bavaria, I see lively festivals that truly capture the character of the place. Bavarian folk traditions and festivals are an important aspect of the culture, giving tourists a glimpse into the heart and soul of this stunning region. There's a strong sense of community and pride in the air, and the locals take their festivals seriously, whether it's the joyful Fasching (Carnival) or the deeply ingrained local rituals that liven up the streets.

Fasching (carnival)
Fasching, the Bavarian counterpart of Carnival, is one of the most anticipated events in Bavaria, taking place often in the weeks leading up to Lent. In Munich and other Bavarian cities, the streets are alive with bright parades, music, and people dressed in elaborate costumes. The ambiance is upbeat, with a lighthearted vibe that encourages everyone—both locals and tourists—to join in the fun. It's a time when the customary norms of everyday life are eased, allowing individuals to enjoy a carefree, joyous spirit for a short period of time.

The "Weiberfastnacht" (Women's Carnival Day) is the pinnacle of Fasching, when women take charge of the festivities, sometimes even taking over town halls or severing men's connections in a playful show of rebellion. This is followed by days of parades with gigantic floats, dancers, street entertainers, and lots of Bavarian music. If you're visiting Bavaria during this time, don't miss out on the festivities. It's an immersion experience in Bavarian culture, allowing you to see the people's joy and humor.

Traditional Bavarian Music and Dance
Bavarian folk music is an essential component of the cultural fabric. Whether you're in a crowded beer garden or at a local festival, classic Bavarian brass bands are a continuous presence. The music, which is frequently played on instruments such as the trumpet, tuba, and accordion, has a captivating intensity that gets people tapping their feet or even jumping into dancing. The tunes are lively and undeniably Bavarian, and no matter where you are, they instantly foster a sense of community.

One of the most well-known Bavarian dances is the Schuhplattler, a frenetic, foot-stomping traditional dance performed by men and women dressed in bright lederhosen and dirndls. The dancers smack their thighs, knees, and shoes to the beat of the song, resulting in a display that is as much about energy and coordination as it is about Bavarian patriotism. Schuhplattler performances are frequently seen during festivals, particularly in the Alps or rural communities, and are entertaining to watch. And if you're lucky, you might even get invited to participate!

The songs and dances are more than just entertainment; they also celebrate the region's heritage. They've been passed down through the centuries, and each performance or song tells a story—whether it's about celebrating the harvest, commemorating a historical event, or simply bringing the community together. If you have the opportunity, consider attending a dance or a concert at one of the several beer gardens. There's nothing like feeling the pulse of Bavarian folk music and joining a centuries-old tradition.

Local Festivals

Aside from Fasching, Bavaria is home to various local festivals that commemorate anything from harvest time to religious customs. Oktoberfest may be the most well-known, but don't underestimate the appeal of smaller, provincial festivals. Community festivals are held in villages around Bavaria to celebrate the entrance of spring, the harvest, and even the changing of seasons. These gatherings feature local food, homemade items, traditional music, and, of course, plenty of beer. It's not only about the spectacle; these festivities provide a true taste of Bavarian friendliness, with visitors likely to be received like family.

Whether you're in a big city or a tiny village, attending one of these local festivals provides you a better understanding of Bavarian culture. The way locals share their food, music, and time with guests exudes warmth, providing an experience that feels like stepping back in time while being very much present.

The Bavarian Dialect

As I toured Bavaria, I immediately realized that the Bavarian dialect (Bairisch) is more than just a variety of German—it's a completely different universe of sounds and emotions! While Standard German (Hochdeutsch) is commonly spoken throughout Germany, Bavarian has a special charm that allows you to see into the heart of the place. This native dialect has a long history and is inextricably linked to Bavarian culture. Despite the fact that many Bavarians speak both Bavarian and Standard German, you'll frequently hear people switching between the two, especially in rural regions or during casual talks.

How Bavarian differs from Standard German

Bavarian is more than just an accent; it has distinct vocabulary, pronunciations, and grammar that might be difficult for someone fluent in Standard German to understand. In fact, Bavarians joke that other Germans can't always understand every word in a Bavarian discourse.

For example, in Standard German, "Ich habe Hunger" means "I am hungry," yet in Bavarian, you would hear "I hab' Hunger" or even "I hob Hunger." Certain consonants are either softened or altered. The "ch" sound in words like "nicht" (not) or "ich" (I) in Standard German becomes "k" or "g" in Bavarian, transforming "nicht" into "nix."

Another enjoyable aspect is the usage of entirely distinct terminology for everyday objects. For example:

• Standard German: "Kartoffel" (potato).

• Bavarian: "erdäpfel"

• Standard German: "Apfel" (apple).

• Bavarian: "Zierapfel" (a name used occasionally in rural areas).

And it's not just the word; certain expressions have an entirely distinct flavor in Bavarian. While "Guten Morgen" (Good Morning) is understood in both dialects, locals may greet you with a hearty "Grüß Gott!""—literally meaning "God greets you!"" and one of the most common greetings you'll hear around the region.

Common Bavarian Phrases to Engage with Locals

If you intend to spend time in Bavaria, knowing a few Bavarian phrases will not only help you navigate conversations, but will also get you some warm smiles from locals. Here are a few helpful sentences to get you started:

• Grüß Gott! - Hi! (Instead of the customary greeting, "Hallo")

• Wia geht's? - How are things going? (Literally, "How's it?")

• Pfiat Di! - Goodbye. (A more Bavarian rendition of "Auf Wiedersehen")

- Is it a net schee? - Isn't it beautiful? (Ideal for expressing awe at the scenery.)

- "I bin aus...- I'm from..."

- Are you coming with me? - Will you join us? (Invite someone to join you).

- Das gibt 's net! - No way! / That is inconceivable! (Used when something is difficult to believe).

- Do you know what? - Do you know what? (A casual technique to initiate a discussion)

- Do you have hunger? - Are you hungry? (Useful when you're ready to eat)

- Please measure! - One liter of beer, please! (Required for ordering at the beer garden!)

While these are only a few instances, they should make you feel more connected to the local culture. And believe me, when you try a little Bavarian, even if it's only a simple "Grüß Gott!" or "Pfiati!", you'll notice the difference in communicating with the pleasant inhabitants who take great pride in their language.

Crafts, Art, and Souvenirs

When I think of Bavarian crafts and souvenirs, I envision elaborate wood carvings, colorful beer steins, and traditional apparel that represents the region's cultural past. Bavaria is a hub of talent and craftsmanship, and I've discovered some genuinely one-of-a-kind items that make ideal souvenirs or gifts.

Handmade Wood Carvings

Bavarian wood carvings are among the most treasured gifts you can find here. You can find them in shops all across the country, particularly in mountain towns like Mittenwald and Oberammergau, which are recognized for their long-standing woodcarving traditions. The intricate craftsmanship of these wooden miniatures, which frequently portray scenes from Bavarian life or wildlife, is impressive. From little animal figurines to huge statues, they convey a feeling of Bavarian history and environment. During one of my trips, I picked up a hand-carved cuckoo clock, which I will keep forever for its beauty as well as the memory it holds.

Beer Steins

If there is one Bavarian memento that encapsulates the essence of the place, it is the beer stein. These classic mugs, typically made of stoneware, pewter, or ceramic, come in a variety of sizes and styles. Some are wonderfully painted with classic Bavarian landscapes, while others have exquisite engravings or pewter covers. For me, acquiring a beer stein is like embracing a piece of Bavaria's beer culture, especially when you consider how deeply rooted beer-drinking is in local traditions. Whether you choose a classic or more modern style, a beer stein is a great way to remember your experience at the region's vibrant beer gardens.

Traditional Bavarian Clothing
Bavarian attire is another treasured keepsake. Locals wear the famed lederhosen for men and dirndls for women at festivals like Oktoberfest and traditional festivities, and they can be purchased in numerous places. These outfits are of superior quality and craftsmanship. The leather used for lederhosen is tough but comfortable, and the intricate embroidery on dirndls reflects the region's cultural pride. Even if you don't intend to wear them to a festival, owning a piece of Bavarian costume is a terrific way to capture some of the local character. I've always enjoyed the sense of history that these costumes evoke, and putting into

a dirndl or lederhosen transports me back to the Bavarian festivals I've attended.

Other Local Crafts

Aside from wood carvings and apparel, I recommend looking at Bavarian pottery and textiles. Ceramics created in towns such as Waldsassen are well-known for their bright glazes and classic designs. Similarly, woven textiles, such as the well-known Bavarian blankets, which are generally made of wool, make excellent useful and artistic keepsakes. These pieces represent the region's dedication to exceptional craftsmanship and are ideal for bringing a touch of Bavarian charm into your house.

Chapter 5: Outdoor Adventures and Natural Beauty

Hiking in the Bavarian Alps

Hiking in the Bavarian Alps is an experience unlike any other. The scenery is simply stunning, with snow-capped peaks, lush valleys, and crystal-clear lakes. Whether you're an experienced mountaineer or a casual hiker, there are trails that will capture you, with some of the most breathtaking vistas in Europe.

Best Trails, Peak Hikes, and Scenic Views

One of the best aspects of hiking in the Bavarian Alps is the sheer variety of trails, each with its own distinct experience. Here are a handful I strongly suggest.

Zugspitze is Germany's Highest Peak

If you want to test your limits, the Zugspitze hike should be at the top of your list. Zugspitze, at 2,962 meters, is Germany's highest summit. The trail from Eibsee Lake is a difficult ascent, but the reward is well worth it. The top offers spectacular views that span across the Alps to Austria and Switzerland. If you want a more leisurely experience, take the Zugspitze cable car to the top.

Partnach Gorge, Eckbauer

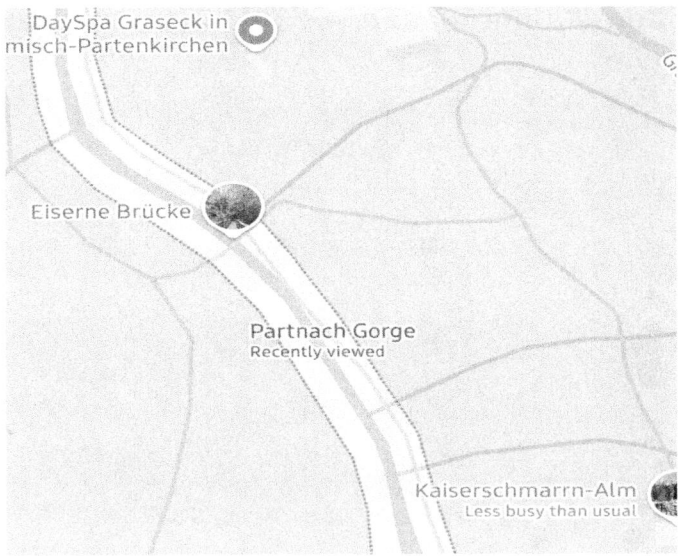

This trail near Garmisch-Partenkirchen offers a moderate hike with a variety of scenery, including waterfalls, spectacular cliffs, and alpine meadows. The Partnach Gorge is a breathtaking natural wonder, with walking pathways that lead you along rushing waters and over tight, towering rock formations. After exploring the gorge, continue hiking towards Eckbauer for even more breathtaking views of the surrounding hills.

Höllentalklamm and the Höllentalferner Glacier

The Höllental Gorge and its glacier walk are another hidden gem in the Garmisch-Partenkirchen area that will make your heart race. The canyon is a stunning, meandering trail formed through steep rock walls, while the glacier trek provides a close-up glimpse of the Höllentalferner Glacier. The walk is rather tough, but it takes you to one of the most spectacular and scenic areas in the Alps.

Königssee and Watzmann Mountains

One of Bavaria's most renowned vistas is the beautiful Königssee, which is flanked by high mountains. A trek around the lake will lead you to some of the area's most breathtaking views, including the Watzmann mountain range. This hike allows you to explore dense forests, meadows, and stunning scenery while listening to the soothing sounds of the lake's water.

Alpenvorland Trail

If you don't want to do a complete mountain ascent but yet want to see amazing vistas, the Alpenvorland Trail might be the best option. This easy-to-moderate track runs along the Alps' foothills, offering beautiful views of the towering peaks to the south. Along the route, you'll pass through picturesque Bavarian villages and get a personal look at local culture.

Essential Gear and Preparation Tips

When hiking in the Bavarian Alps, planning is essential for a safe and fun trip. Here are some recommendations and necessary equipment I recommend:

Footwear
A solid pair of hiking footwear with adequate ankle support is required. The paths, particularly those leading to higher elevations, can be rough, slippery, and steep, so you'll need footwear that can handle a wide range of terrain.

Weather-appropriate Clothing
Even during the warmer months, the weather in the Alps may be unpredictable. I always advocate wearing moisture-wicking layers that allow you to adjust to temperature variations. A light, breathable base layer, an insulating mid-layer, and a waterproof outer shell will keep you warm whether you're trekking through a balmy valley or on a cold mountaintop.

Navigation Tools
While many paths are well-marked, it is always advisable to bring a map or GPS equipment. A portable power bank can also help keep your phone charged on longer walks.

Water and Snacks

The alpine climate can be dry, and climbing at high altitudes can cause dehydration faster than you'd anticipate. Be sure to bring lots of water, especially on longer hikes. Energy snacks such as nuts, granola bars, and fruit can keep you energized and ready for the next stretch.

Sunscreen and Sunglasses
Even on cloudy days, sunlight can be intense at higher elevations. I never go hiking without sunscreen and a good pair of UV-blocking sunglasses to protect my eyes.

Emergency Kit
Always prepare for the unexpected. A simple first-aid kit with bandages, pain medications, and blister treatment can make all the difference. A whistle, torch, and multitool are also useful equipment to have.

Weather Check
Before you leave, check the weather forecast. The weather in the Alps is unpredictable, and storms can arrive swiftly. If the outlook is bad, consider postponing your hike or choosing a lower-altitude trail.

Cycling In Bavaria

Cycling in Bavaria is one of the most enjoyable ways to explore this stunning region. From meandering roads along gorgeous rivers to calm trails through lush forests, biking here provides the ideal balance of nature, culture, and adventure. Whether you're an expert cyclist or just seeking a relaxing ride, Bavaria's well-maintained bike routes accommodate all skill levels, allowing you to explore the environment at your own pace.

Cycle Routes Along Rivers and Through Forests

Bavaria's bike routes are among the most scenic in Europe, particularly those that follow its famed rivers, such as the Danube, Isar and Main. These rivers offer not only breathtaking views, but also a flat, easy ride, making them ideal for people new to cycling or seeking a relaxing journey. You'll pass through lovely towns, picturesque villages, and lush green landscapes while following the water's natural flow.

One of my favorite routes is along the Isar River, which runs from the Bavarian Alps to Munich. The path leads through woodlands and meadows, with plenty of options to pause for a swim or a picnic by the river. Another highlight is the Danube cycle trail, which combines tranquil riverbanks, rolling hills, and historic sites such as Regensburg and Passau, where you may visit medieval architecture in between biking sessions.

If you like woodland paths, there are various options in the Bavarian Forest National Park. These pathways lead you through lush woodlands, providing an opportunity to connect with nature while cycling in a peaceful setting. Keep a watch out for fauna, such as deer and wild boar, as well as the breathtaking vegetation that defines this old woodland.

Tips for Renting Bikes and Navigating Rural Routes
Renting a bike in Bavaria is simple, especially in major cities like Munich, Nuremberg, and Regensburg, where numerous rental shops provide everything from regular city bikes to e-bikes and mountain bikes for more rough paths. To ensure availability during peak tourist season (spring through autumn), I strongly advise you to book your bike ahead of time.

When traveling rural routes, a good map or app is vital, as some of the more distant trails may not be properly marked. I particularly enjoy utilizing apps like Komoot or Google Maps for bicycle routes because they provide specific information on terrain, difficulty level, and projected trip time. Many bike rental companies also include maps of popular cycling routes, so don't hesitate to request one when you pick up your bike.

If you're cycling on country roads, make sure you're prepared to navigate through quieter, less-trafficked areas. While these routes often provide the most gorgeous and quiet experiences, you may encounter narrow roads or more difficult climbs, so know your limits. If you're not in the mood for a difficult ride, there are lots of e-bike alternatives available that will allow you to experience the beauty of Bavaria without having to worry about elevation gain.

Practical Tips for Cyclists

Safety First
Wear a helmet at all times, even if the law does not mandate it. Some of the trails are bumpy, so it's best to stay safe.

Pack Light

Bring only what you need for the day: water, food, sunscreen, and a tiny first-aid kit. Bavaria's weather can be unpredictable, so bring a light jacket or rain gear.

Respect the Local Traffic Rules
Cyclists share the road with automobiles in some regions, therefore be careful of local road signs and allow pedestrians the right of way when cycling through villages and towns.

Timing Your Ride
If you're visiting a major tourist area, try to ride early in the morning or late in the day to avoid crowds and get the ideal lighting for photography.

Bicycle Repair
Always keep a basic repair kit on hand, which should include a spare tube, tire levers, and a pump. Bike shops are very common in major cities, however it is always advisable to be prepared.

Bavarian Lakes and Water Activities

Some of my favorite recollections of Bavaria are its beautiful lakes. These sparkling pools of water are more than just beautiful; they also provide a variety of activities to help you relax and connect with nature. Whether you're sailing across a tranquil lake, swimming, or strolling along the coastline, Bavaria's lakes have something for every visitor.

Bodensee (Lake Constance)

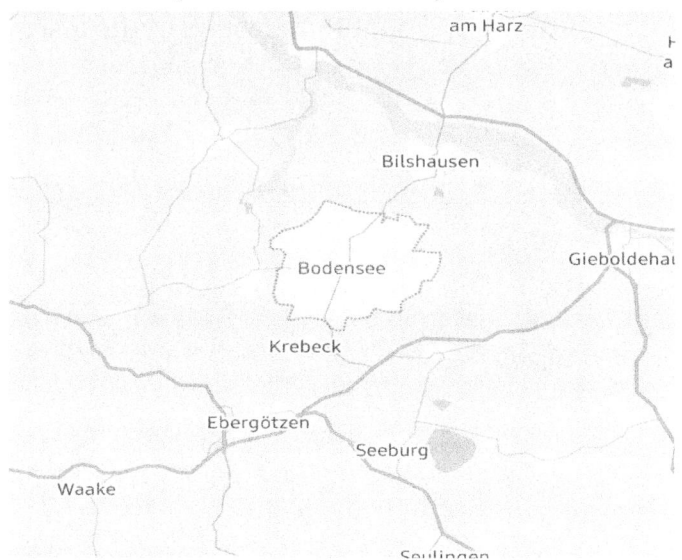

Lake Constance, often known as Bodensee, is one of Bavaria's most magnificent lakes. It's a water lover's heaven, spanning Germany, Austria, and Switzerland. The crystal-clear lake is ideal for boating and swimming, and I couldn't pass up hiring a paddle boat on a beautiful summer day. The lake's peaceful waters are bordered by rolling hills and attractive lakeside towns, making it the perfect location for a quiet day.

I definitely recommend visiting Lindau, which sits on the lake's shore. It feels like you've stepped into a storybook with its lovely medieval buildings and colorful waterfront. You may also take a ferry to the flower island of Mainau, which is known for its stunning gardens and panoramic views of the lake.

Chiemsee - The Bavarian Sea

Chiemsee, sometimes known as the "Bavarian Sea," is another beautiful lake worth investigating. Known for its size and stunning alpine backdrop, I took a relaxing boat ride across the lake to visit the impressive Herrenchiemsee Palace, also known as the "Bavarian Versailles." The island where the palace is located is tranquil and scenic, with plenty of walking paths and spots to appreciate the beauty.

Chiemsee's crystal-clear waters are ideal for a refreshing plunge, especially in the summer. The lake's beaches are well-kept, making it an ideal location for families to spend the day by the water.

Königssee: The Jewel of the Bavarian Alps

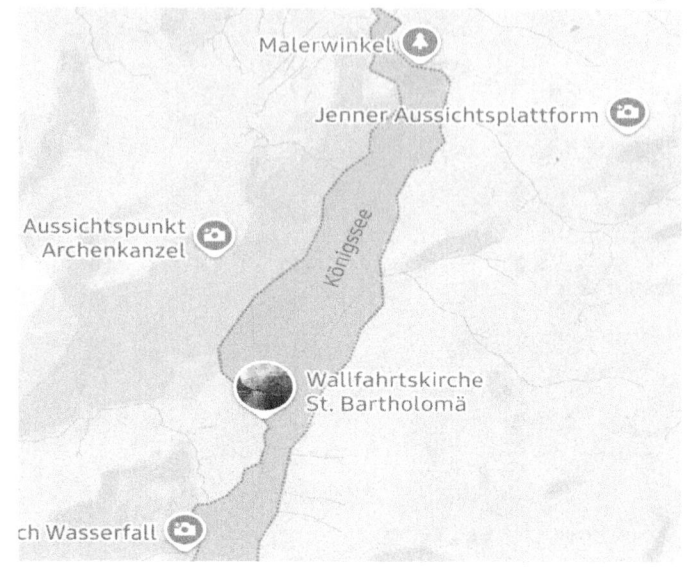

One of the most memorable experiences I had in Bavaria was seeing Königssee, a stunning lake tucked deep in the Bavarian Alps. The lake is surrounded by towering cliffs, and its emerald green waters are so transparent that you can see the rocks beneath the surface. I took a boat tour to the famed St. Bartholomä church, a gorgeous place on the lake's edge that is only accessible by boat.

Königssee is a paradise for nature enthusiasts, with several chances for water activities. I had a relaxing afternoon kayaking, gliding over the tranquil waters surrounded by mountains. For those who prefer to keep dry, there are numerous walking and hiking trails that provide stunning views of the lake and its surroundings.

Lakeside Towns and Beach Resorts
The lakes of Bavaria offer more than just the water; the cities and resorts that line their shores are equally appealing. Take a leisurely stroll along the lakeside promenade in Garmisch-Partenkirchen, or visit the picturesque town of Prien, where you may relax at a lakeside cafe or explore the neighboring nature reserves.

For a more resort-like experience, I recommend visiting the area around Lake Tegernsee, where I discovered stunning lakeside resorts complete with spas, wellness centers, and outdoor pools that overlook the water. There's nothing like relaxing in a hot tub while admiring the scenery of the surrounding Alps.

Winter Activities in the Alps

If you enjoy the excitement of the slopes and the crisp, pure air of the mountains, Bavaria's Bavarian Alps provide some of the best winter sports experiences available. Whether you're an avid skier, a snowboarder, or someone who prefers the peace and quiet of cross-country skiing, Bavaria has it all. The Alps are a popular winter sports destination due to its breathtaking alpine landscape, world-class facilities, and inviting environment.

Ski Resorts in the Bavarian Alps
The Bavarian Alps are home to several renowned ski resorts where you can ski, snowboard, and enjoy the breathtaking vistas of snow-covered peaks. Garmisch-Partenkirchen is a well-known resort that not only has Germany's tallest mountain, Zugspitze, but also provides world-class skiing, snowboarding, and après-ski activities. The resort is well-equipped with contemporary lifts, long runs, and facilities for both beginners and advanced skiers.

Berchtesgaden, noted for its breathtaking landscapes and the Königssee lake, is another excellent choice for skiing in a more peaceful, less crowded setting. Oberstdorf, located in the Allgäu Alps, provides a combination of downhill and cross-country skiing, as well as breathtaking views of the valleys underneath.

The greatest time to visit is from mid-December to March, when the snow conditions are optimal. However, other resorts, such as

Garmisch-Partenkirchen, provide skiing well into the spring due to their high-altitude slopes.

Snowboarding and Terrain Park
The Alps are not only for classic skiing. If you enjoy snowboarding, there are lots of slopes and terrain parks to explore. Garmisch-Partenkirchen has an excellent snowboarding culture, with a range of freestyle terrain and parks to suit even the most daring riders. Oberstdorf is also gaining popularity for snowboarding, with slopes designed for both novices and those looking for more challenging runs.

The snowboarding community in the Bavarian Alps is active and supportive, with various resorts providing snowboarding training and specialized events such as snowboarding championships. If you're a beginner, several resorts offer first-timer packages to help you hit the slopes confidently.

Cross-Country Skiing
If you prefer the peace and quiet of snow-covered forests and valleys, cross-country skiing is a fantastic way to explore the Bavarian Alps. This type of skiing is an excellent workout and provides a slower, more intimate connection with nature. Kochel am See and Tegernsee are ideal

cross-country skiing destinations, with well-maintained trails winding through some of Bavaria's most gorgeous scenery. Berchtesgaden National Park also features some of the best cross-country skiing trails, with vistas of jagged mountain peaks and calm valleys.

Many of the region's ski resorts include groomed cross-country ski trails suitable for both beginners and experienced skiers. Cross-country skiing is a really peaceful activity due to its slow pace and beautiful natural settings.

Preparing for Cold Weather Activities
Winter in the Bavarian Alps can be both intense and magical, so planning ahead of time is essential for a memorable and safe experience. Here's what you should know.

Dress with Layers
The weather in the mountains is unpredictable. I usually suggest wearing a moisture-wicking base layer, an insulating layer, and a waterproof outer layer. To stay warm during breaks, remember to bring your gloves, hat, and scarf.

Equipment Rental

Most resorts in the Bavarian Alps have high-quality equipment rentals, so you do not need to carry your own gear unless you choose to. If you are new to winter sports, renting equipment is an excellent way to get started.

Know Your Limits
Whether you're skiing, snowboarding, or cross-country skiing, recognize your skill level and stay within it. There are slopes for all ability levels, so start slowly and seek professional tuition if you're new to the sport.

Stay Hydrated and Energized
The cold air can dry you faster than you think, so drink plenty of water. Keep some food in your backpack so you can refuel while on the road.

Weather Conditions
Always check the weather before going out. The weather in the mountains can be unpredictable, so plan for snowstorms, fog, or even sunny moments.

Wildlife and Nature Reserves

When I think about Bavaria's natural beauty, I immediately think of its huge vistas, high Alps, and untouched wilderness areas. The region is home to two of Germany's most beautiful national parks, Berchtesgaden National Park and Bayerischer Wald National Park, both of which are havens for wildlife aficionados and nature lovers like myself.

Berchtesgaden National Park

Berchtesgaden National Park, located in the Bavarian Alps near the Austrian border, is a real gem. It is one of Germany's oldest and best-preserved national parks, with over 200 square kilometers of rocky mountains, crystal-clear lakes, and deep forests. The park is a wildlife paradise, and as I went along its paths, I was fortunate enough to get glimpses of the elusive golden eagle soaring high above the valley. If you get up early, you're likely to see chamois (wild goats), red deer, and even a roe deer grazing calmly along the forest border.

The highlight for me was wandering along Königssee Lake, a stunning emerald-green lake flanked by sheer cliffs. White-tailed eagles can be seen gracefully skimming across the lake. The calm scenery and quiet pathways provided some of my most relaxing times in Bavaria.

If you enjoy hiking, there are several spectacular paths across the park, including the Watzmann Mountain track, which allows you to challenge yourself to top Germany's third-highest mountain.

Bayerischer Wald Nationalpark

Bayerischer Wald National Park, Germany's first national park, is located just a short drive from the Czech border. This park, which covers more than 24,000 hectares, is a biodiversity hotspot. I liked how it's one of the few areas in Europe where nature is allowed to evolve without human interference. It is an area where trees and meadows live in their most natural state.

What actually distinguishes Bayerischer Wald is its commitment to establishing a wildlife-friendly habitat. Animal tracking trails throughout the park provide opportunities to learn about the area's wildlife through interactive displays and guided tours. I was fortunate to see wild boars, lynxes, and even the beautiful European bison, which were once on the brink of extinction. The park also has a wolf refuge, where visitors can see these intriguing carnivores in their natural environment.

For nature treks, I highly recommend the Baumwipfelpfad (Tree Top Walk), an elevated pathway that leads through the park's canopy and provides breathtaking panoramic views of the neighboring Bavarian landscape. It's an incredible experience that provides a unique perspective on the forest below.

Wildlife Watching and Nature Walks

Both of these parks provide excellent chances for wildlife viewing and nature walks. There is something for everyone, whether you enjoy birdwatching, monitoring animals, or simply relaxing in the tranquil splendor of the forests. Walking along the well-marked trails in both parks allowed me to witness the changing seasons—spring and summer brought bursts of color, while autumn changed the landscape into a patchwork of golds and reds.

When hiking in these parks, maintain a respectful distance from the wildlife. The animals here are wild, and they should be permitted to roam without being disturbed. However, if you are patient and quiet, you may be lucky enough to observe a wild boar, red fox, or perhaps a black grouse dashing through the underbrush.

Chapter 6: Shopping and Souvenirs

Shopping in Munich and Nuremberg

When it comes to shopping, Munich and Nuremberg have something for everyone. Whether you're looking for luxury items, interesting souvenirs, or real local products, these two cities provide a diverse shopping experience that combines current flair with Bavarian history.

Luxury Shopping in Munich
Munich is a premium shopping destination, and if you're looking for designer stores and high-end

fashion, then right to Maximilianstrasse. This is where you can find high-end brands like Gucci, Louis Vuitton, and Prada, as well as fine jewelry boutiques and exclusive galleries. The street itself is a work of beauty, with stunning historic architecture serving as the ideal backdrop for your luxury shopping binge.

If you want a more casual shopping experience, Kaufingerstrasse and Neuhauserstrasse provide a mix of well-known global brands and Bavarian merchants. You can shop for everything from German fashion to electronic gadgets all within walking distance of Munich's iconic Marienplatz.

Traditional markets in Munich and Nuremberg
For a taste of traditional Bavarian shopping, head to Munich's Viktualienmarkt, a bustling open-air food market in the city center. Fresh produce and local cheeses are among the items available here, as are gourmet meats, honey, and handcrafted crafts. It's the ideal spot to find unique souvenirs and enjoy some of the best regional products. Don't forget to visit the kiosks selling Lebkuchen (traditional gingerbread) and homemade pretzels for a true flavor of Bayern.

The Handwerkerhof is a lovely medieval-style market located below Nuremberg's city walls. This area is full of workshops where you can observe local artisans at work, and the stores sell anything from leather goods to hand-carved wooden toys and traditional beer steins. It's a wonderful place to find a one-of-a-kind present that genuinely embodies the region's craftsmanship.

Hidden Gems of Shopping in Munich
While the big shopping districts are excellent, I've discovered a few hidden treasures in Munich that are worth checking out. Sendlinger Strasse is a charming retail route with a variety of boutique shops and artisanal stores. You can find unusual fashion items, vintage stores, and eccentric accessories that you won't find anywhere else. It's an excellent spot for wandering and discovering Munich's less touristy side.

Isartor, which is home to small galleries, design businesses, and local fashion boutiques, is another often-overlooked destination. It's a calmer section of the city, yet it's brimming with riches.

Local Products to Bring Home
When it comes to shopping for local items, there are a few Bavarian specialties that you simply must

miss. One of my favorites is Bavarian cheese, specifically those from the Allgäu region. Whether you're looking for creamy Obatzda (a soft cheese spread) or rich, aged cheeses, there are plenty of alternatives to dazzle your friends and family.

Bavarian honey is another delicious treat. Local honey, particularly from the countryside, is frequently infused with the aromas of wildflowers and herbs, making it an ideal souvenir for anyone who appreciates a sweet and natural gift.

And, of course, no trip to Bavaria is complete without bringing back some local beer. Craft beers from small, family-run breweries are widely available throughout the region. Purchase a few bottles of Weißbier (wheat beer), or try other options such as Pilsner or Dunkel. Don't forget to acquire a traditional beer stein—it's a terrific way to remember your stay in Bavaria.

Bavarian Marketplaces

When I think about Bavaria, one of the first things that comes to mind is its vivid markets, which are filled with life, color, and history. Whether you're meandering around the famous Christmas markets during the holiday season or browsing flea markets all year, shopping in Bavaria feels like stepping into a novel, full of unique finds and local treasures.

Christmas Markets

Bavaria is famous for its Christmas markets, which wonderfully capture the charm of the holiday season. From the end of November to December, towns and cities around the region come alive with dazzling lights, the aroma of roasted chestnuts and mulled wine, and the sound of cherry carolers. Munich's Christkindlesmarkt, located in the city centre at Marienplatz, is possibly the most well-known, with its attractive wooden kiosks selling anything from handcrafted ornaments to locally baked gingerbread cookies. There's something magical about meandering among the snow-covered kiosks, sipping warm Glühwein (mulled wine), and looking for the ideal handcrafted present.

But Munich is not the only destination to visit Bavarian Christmas markets. Nuremberg's Christkindlesmarkt is world-renowned and draws tourists from all over the world. Nuremberg's medieval setting adds to its charm, with stalls selling beautifully crafted toys, hand-carved wooden figures, and the iconic Nuremberg gingerbread, "Lebkuchen." I highly recommend stopping by one of the food stalls to try these iconic treats—they're unlike anything I've ever tasted.

For a more intimate experience, visit smaller cities such as Rothenburg ob der Tauber or Bamberg, where the markets are equally enchanting but in a more relaxed setting. The historic architecture of these villages adds to their beauty, making you feel as if you've stepped back in time.

Flea Markets
While Christmas markets are seasonal, Bavaria's flea markets are open year-round. If you enjoy vintage products, antiques, or unique treasures, you're in for a treat. Munich's largest flea market, hosted at the Theresienwiese (the same location as Oktoberfest), is an excellent place to look for one-of-a-kind items such as second-hand clothing, rare books, and vintage furniture. It's like a gigantic treasure hunt, and I always find something unusual, whether it's a typical Bavarian stein or a finely carved antique clock.

Nuremberg also has a beautiful flea market called the "Flöhmärkte" (flea market), which sells a variety of collectibles, vintage things, and handcrafted goods. If you enjoy art, the flea markets in Munich and Regensburg are great places to find local paintings and prints, frequently by emerging Bavarian artists.

Local Crafts
Bavaria is rich in workmanship, and the markets are an excellent place to get locally crafted goods that represent the region's history. Artisans sell everything from intricately carved wooden figures to hand-blown glass ornaments. One of my favorite purchases was a collection of handcrafted Bavarian dolls clothed in traditional lederhosen and dirndls, which make an excellent keepsake.

If you enjoy traditional dress, you must take home a piece of Bavarian garb. Lederhosen (leather shorts) and dirndls (traditional dresses) are available in a variety of markets, and the quality is excellent. I've purchased several handmade dirndls from local vendors and enjoy how they embody the essence of Bavarian culture.

Consider purchasing a smaller but equally remarkable piece of Bavarian pottery, such as a hand-painted beer mug or a decorative plate with mountain scenes. I've also discovered beautifully carved wooden toys, which are ideal for children or as a delightful display item.

Top Picks for Unique Finds

Handmade Bavarian Pretzel Baskets
If you enjoy Bavarian pretzels (and who doesn't?), pick up a handwoven basket to carry your snack in style.

Local Cheese and Charcuterie
Many markets offer locally made cheeses, sausages, and cured meats. It's the ideal way to bring a piece of Bavaria home—or to enjoy it right away.

Traditional Bavarian Beer Steins
These handcrafted mugs are not just souvenirs; they are pieces of Bavarian heritage. Whether you choose an extravagant collector's item or a simpler design, every drink will bring back memories of your Bavarian vacation.

Bavarian Jewelry
I discovered several exquisite pieces of jewelry at Munich's Viktualienmarkt, with elaborate designs inspired by Bavarian folklore and environment. It's a fantastic opportunity to bring home a wearable piece of the place.

Traditional Clothing and Apparel

When you think about Bavaria, one of the first things that springs to mind is probably the classic Lederhosen and Dirndl. These traditional Bavarian clothes are more than simply apparel; they represent Bavarian pride and culture and are proudly worn during festivals, special events, and in everyday life, particularly in the countryside. As someone who has spent time entrenched in Bavarian culture, I can tell you that wearing these clothing is like embracing the region's own heartbeat.

Lederhosen and Dirndls Are A Timeless Tradition

Lederhosen, men's leather shorts or pants, and Dirndl, women's lovely dress, have long been part of Bavarian heritage. Lederhosen were traditionally worn by men working in agriculture or forestry, making them ideal for the harsh outdoor lifestyle. The Dirndl, on the other hand, was traditionally worn by women in rural Bavaria as a utilitarian yet stylish garment for daily tasks.

Both outfits have become synonymous with Bavarian celebrations, particularly Oktoberfest. At this world-famous beer festival, individuals of all ages proudly wear these garments, whether in a tiny beer garden or inside the big beer tent. It's more than simply the fashion; it's a celebration of Bavarian culture.

Where to buy Authentic Bavarian Attire
If you want to buy your own Lederhosen or Dirndl, there are various shops throughout Bavaria where you may get genuine pieces. Munich is home to some of the most well-known Bavarian clothing stores, especially during Oktoberfest season. Hirsch Moden is one of the most well-known stores, offering high-quality Lederhosen made of premium leather, as well as finely handmade Dirndls with elaborate embroidery and traditional detailing.

For a more genuine, intimate experience, I recommend stopping by smaller, local shops in Bavarian cities like Garmisch-Partenkirchen or Nuremberg. These locations frequently include one-of-a-kind, handcrafted copies of traditional clothes. In fact, some smaller boutiques offer special tailoring, guaranteeing that your Dirndl or Lederhosen fits exactly, making it a true Bavarian gem.

Trachtenmoden, a series of traditional garment boutiques located throughout Bavaria, is another popular option. They provide a diverse choice of styles, from budget-friendly to premium pieces, guaranteeing that there is something for everyone's budget and taste.

Modern Perspectives on Traditional Bavarian Fashion

While the classic Lederhosen and Dirndl remain symbols of Bavarian culture, contemporary interpretations of traditional attire have begun to develop. Many fashion designers are combining traditional Bavarian components with current styles to create a fresh take on the classic look. Dirndl-inspired dresses, for example, have become popular in metropolitan contexts. These dresses, frequently with lower hemlines or contemporary fabrics, have gained popularity among young women, particularly in locations such as Munich.

Similarly, Lederhosen are no longer just for beer festivals. I've noticed that many Bavarians, especially younger generations, wear modernized Lederhosen, which are frequently matched with stylish blouses or coats. During the summer months, you may see these clothes at casual gatherings, picnics, or even the office, giving them a more everyday appeal.

Fashion firms in Bavaria have also begun to experiment with combining classic fabrics like wool, gingham checks, and leather with modern designs and colors. Many of these pieces can be found at the annual Munich Trachten Fashion Show, when designers show off their latest takes on Bavarian flair. It's amazing to see how the traditional can meet the modern, and this mix gives a fresh, youthful vibe to what was formerly regarded to be a special event garment.

Why should you Embrace Bavarian Fashion?
Wearing traditional Bavarian clothes means more than just looking good; it also means identifying with the region's culture, legacy, and history. When I first wore my own set of Lederhosen to Oktoberfest, I felt a stronger connection to those around me. It was as if I had become a part of something far bigger—a long-standing tradition passed down through generations.

Gifts and Gourmet Delights

When I visit Bavaria, I am always on the search for unique native cuisine presents and mementos to take home. Whether for a loved one or as a personal treat, Bavarian gifts are an excellent way to share a bit of this stunning region with others. Here are some of my favorite edible mementos and the best places to get them.

Local Food Gifts

Bavarian Chocolates
Bavarian chocolates are a must-try while visiting the region, and they make ideal gifts for anybody with a sweet taste. One of my favorites is the traditional Bayerische Pralinen, which are beautiful, handcrafted pralines filled with everything from hazelnut cream to fruit-infused ganaches. Artisanal chocolates are available from brands such as Kaffekommune in Munich, as well as small, family-owned chocolatiers throughout Bavaria's lovely towns. I enjoy picking up a box as a lovely memory of my vacations!

Bavarian Mustard
Bavarian mustard, especially the mittelscharf (medium hot) version, is another traditional present. It is known for its silky texture and excellent combination of tanginess and spice, and it goes well with Bavarian sausages, pretzels, and pork. Many local markets sell mustard jars in a range of tastes, ranging from sweet to spicy. I discovered the most delicious mustards at Munich's

Viktualienmarkt, where you can also chat with local merchants and try different varieties before making a purchase.

Local Wines
While Bavaria is better known for its beer, it also has a long history of wine production, particularly in Franconia. The Bocksbeutel, a one-of-a-kind, circular wine bottle, houses some of the region's finest wines, such as Silvaner, Riesling, and Müller-Thurgau. I enjoy buying up a bottle (or two!) of locally produced wine as a gift. One of my favorite wine shops is in the picturesque town of Würzburg, which is famed for its wine cellars and vineyards. If you enjoy wine, don't miss this stop.

Best Stores for Souvenirs and Artisanal Goods

Viktualienmarkt, Munich
No vacation to Munich is complete without a stop at the legendary Viktualienmarkt, one of the city's oldest and most recognizable marketplaces. While you're here, you'll find a diverse assortment of Bavarian food presents, including fresh cheeses, sausages, honey and pickles. The market also has modest artisan stores that sell wonderfully crafted wooden toys, delicate pottery, and hand-woven

textiles. It's ideal for finding one-of-a-kind, high-quality souvenirs that showcase Bavarian craftsmanship.

Stadtmuseum Shop, Munich
For something more cultural, I enjoy visiting the museum stores in Munich, particularly those at the Stadtmuseum. You'll find a variety of intriguing products here, including vintage-style Bavarian folk art and literature about local history. The store sells artisan products from local manufacturers, such as elegantly embroidered linens and carved wood objects. I always leave with something memorable that transports me back to the heart of Munich.

German Switzerland, Bamberg
If you travel to the Franconian region, Bamberg is a hidden treasure for artisanal goods. The beautiful stores in this UNESCO World Heritage city are brimming with one-of-a-kind treasures like hand-carved wood sculptures, locally created pottery, and intricate lacework. I always visit Franken Textil, where they sell lovely woolen scarves and gloves that make wonderful, comfortable gifts. The region is particularly well-known for its Rauchbier, a smoked beer, so grabbing a bottle to take home is always a wise decision.

Chapter 7: Practical Information and Tips

Local Laws and Regulations

When traveling Bavaria, it is critical to become acquainted with the local rules and regulations to guarantee a smooth and enjoyable experience. While Bavaria is recognized for its friendly culture, following the local rules will help you blend in and prevent unneeded issues. Here are some important facts concerning driving, drinking, and general cultural customs in Bavaria.

Driving in Bavaria

Bavaria is home to Germany's famous Autobahn, which includes parts with no speed limits. However, this does not imply that you should drive dangerously. Here are some crucial driving laws to remember:

Speed Limits

While some sections of the Autobahn have no speed limits, the majority of highways and city streets have stringent speed limits. The speed limit in urban areas is often 50 km/h (31 mph), whereas on country roads it is normally 100 km/h (62 mph). Always pay attention to the signs, as speed limits are clearly marked.

Alcohol and Driving

Germany has strong regulations around drinking and driving. For most drivers, the legal blood alcohol concentration (BAC) level is 0.05%; however, for new drivers (less than two years of driving experience) and young drivers under the age of 21, the limit is 0.00%. Fines and penalties for exceeding the limit can be severe, so avoid drinking if you intend to drive. Police are known to conduct random breathalyzer tests, particularly during holiday seasons or large gatherings.

Seatbelts and Mobile Phones

Seatbelts are required for all passengers, including the driver. Fines for not using a seatbelt can be high. Using a cell phone while driving without a hands-free system is banned and will result in penalties and points on your driver's license.

Parking

Parking laws are severely enforced, particularly in major towns such as Munich. Always park in approved areas and check for parking signs. Fines for improper parking can accumulate quickly, and your vehicle may be towed.

Drinking Laws and Customs

Bavarians are recognized for their love of beer, and it is an important element of their culture. However, there are a few regulations to follow when having a drink:

Drinking Age

In Bavaria, the legal drinking age is 16 for beer and wine and 18 for spirits (liquor). Keep in mind that if you're under 18, you won't be able to purchase hard liquor, but you might be able to enjoy a beer or wine.

Drinking in Public
Public drinking is typically allowed in Bavaria. People often drink beer in parks or while roaming around the city. However, there are some areas where drinking is restricted, such as near schools or public transportation stops. To avoid a fine, follow local guidelines.

Bavarian Beer Culture
Beer is essential to Bavarian culture. If you're invited to a beer garden or festival, such as Munich's famous Oktoberfest, there are certain rules to obey. When clinking beers, make eye contact and raise your glass ("Prost!") and remember to show respect when drinking with locals.

Cultural Laws and Customs
Bavarians are proud of their traditions, and while their rituals may appear similar to other parts of Germany, they also have their own cultural rules and practices that you should be aware of.

Punctuality is Key
Germans, particularly Bavarians, value punctuality. Arriving on time, whether for a business meeting, a social function, or a dinner reservation, demonstrates respect. If you are running late,

please contact your host or the appropriate person in advance.

Dress Codes
While Bavaria is largely informal, certain occasions, particularly when visiting churches or attending formal events, necessitate modest and respectful clothes. If you intend to visit a church or monastery, dress modestly. Traditional Bavarian garb, such as lederhosen for men and dirndls for women, is frequently worn at Oktoberfest, but it is not required.

Respect for Traditions
Bavarians value their local traditions and believe that cultural customs should be respected. This includes knowing the significance of their traditional events, such as Oktoberfest, and adhering to any specific guidelines imposed by local authorities.

Environmental Awareness
Bavaria is one of Germany's most environmentally concerned areas, with strict recycling legislation. Prepare to properly separate your rubbish: plastics, paper, glass, and general waste all go into individual bins. You may also come across a deposit system for bottles and cans, in which you pay a

modest deposit when purchasing beverages in bottles, which you can reclaim by returning them to specified reverse vending machines.

Smoking Laws

Smoking is forbidden in most public locations in Bavaria, including restaurants, bars, and public transportation. There are designated smoking spots where you can light up, so check for them to avoid penalties. The prohibition is tightly enforced, and there are severe penalties for smoking in restricted places.

Money, Currency and Banking

When it comes to handling money in Bavaria, you'll find it's rather simple, but a little preparation can go a long way toward making your trip more enjoyable. Here's all you need to know about the currency, how to exchange money, and how to stay within your budget when visiting this stunning region.

Currency and ATM

The euro (€) is the official currency in Bavaria and throughout Germany. If you are traveling from outside the Eurozone, you will need to exchange your home money into Euros. Currency exchange services are easily available at airports, train stations, and banks; however, be aware that conversion rates and costs can vary. I've discovered that it's usually cheaper to exchange currency at a local bank or utilize ATMs with competitive rates than to swap money at airports or exchange bureaus.

Speaking of ATMs, Bavaria has a lot of them, particularly in larger cities like Munich, Nuremberg, and Augsburg. You can withdraw cash with your debit or credit card, but bear in mind that some ATMs may impose a small fee, especially if you use a non-German card. To avoid paying extra costs, always check whether the ATM is part of a bank network (such as Deutsche Bank or Commerzbank).

Credit Card and Payment Methods
Most hotels, restaurants, and stores accept credit cards, but it's always a good idea to have some cash on hand for smaller establishments, markets, or when visiting more rural locations. Mastercard and Visa are the most readily accepted, whereas American Express may not be as popular, particularly in smaller areas.

Mobile payments via systems like Apple Pay and Google Pay are becoming increasingly popular in Bavaria, particularly in larger towns. However, if you travel to smaller towns or rural villages, you may discover that cash is still the favored means of payment, especially in family-run shops, cafes, and local markets.

Tipping Customs
Tipping in Bavaria is traditional but not required, and it is always appreciated. In restaurants, it is customary to round up the bill or leave 5-10% of the entire amount as a tip, depending on the service. For example, if your dinner costs €28, rounding it up to €30 is completely okay. If you are dining in a more luxury establishment, you may leave a little extra.

In cafes and beer gardens, it is customary to offer a little tip (about €1-2), particularly if the service was polite and quick. Tipping in taxis is also customary, frequently rounding up to the nearest Euro or adding a few extra Euros for excellent service.

A tip of €1-2 per night for housekeeping is a pleasant gesture for hotel workers, and €1-2 per bag is customary for bellhops who assist with luggage.

Budgeting Tips

Bavaria can be inexpensive or expensive, depending on where you go and how you organize your trip. In Munich, for example, food, sights, and lodging can be expensive, particularly in the city center. Many Bavarian cities, however, have excellent cheap options if you know where to search.

To save money, try staying in guesthouses or pensions rather than hotels, particularly outside big cities. Dining at local beer gardens or markets, such as Munich's Viktualienmarkt, provides excellent food at moderate costs. Furthermore, many cities provide day passes for public transportation, which might save you money on travel.

Tickets for places like Neuschwanstein Castle should be purchased in advance, particularly during high seasons. Some museums offer discounted admission on specific days of the week; check their websites for any discounts.

Emergency Contacts and Useful Numbers

When traveling in Bavaria, you must be prepared for unforeseen scenarios. Knowing what to do and who to contact in an emergency can mean all the difference. Here's what you need to know about being safe and getting help when you need it.

How to Handle Emergencies

In the event of an emergency, whether it be a medical crisis, theft, or an accident, the following numbers are critical:

Emergency Services (Police, Fire, and Ambulance)

Dial 112. This is the general emergency number for Germany's police, fire, and ambulance services. It is free and may be used from any phone, including mobile phones, even if you do not have a SIM card or data.

Police

If you need to contact the police for non-urgent reasons, such as a missing passport or reporting a crime, dial 110.

Hospitals and Medical Assistance

In the event of a medical emergency, call 112 for an ambulance. Bavaria's healthcare system is well-developed, with numerous hospitals in important towns such as Munich, Nuremberg, and Augsburg. If you're not sure where to go, you can ask your hotel or a local drugstore for advice.

Embassy Assistance

If you are a foreign national in need of consular assistance, contact your country's embassy or consulate. You can typically locate the contact information on your country's embassy website or by conducting a fast Google search. For instance, if you are from the United States, the U.S. The Embassy in Berlin handles emergencies, whereas the British Consulate can help UK individuals.

Practical Tips to Stay Safe

Know Your Surroundings

Whether you're in a bustling city like Munich or a tranquil village in the Bavarian Alps, it's critical to be aware of your surroundings. Keep a watch on your valuables in congested areas like train stations, marketplaces, and festivals. Pickpockets can be an issue, especially in tourist-heavy locations.

Use Trusted Transportation Services

If you intend to travel large distances inside Bavaria or to neighboring regions, choose reputable transportation services like Deutsche Bahn (Germany's national train service) or official taxi firms. Avoid unauthorized taxis and private rides.

Stay Informed about Local Conditions
Bavaria, particularly its Alpine regions, can suffer unexpected weather shifts. Always check the weather forecast before going out for an outdoor activity. Winter snowfall may make roads and paths difficult, so it's best to keep informed about conditions.

Health Insurance
It is usually advisable to purchase travel insurance that covers health, accidents, and unexpected emergencies. Make sure your insurance covers medical treatment, hospital stays, and emergency repatriation if necessary. If you live in the EU, your European Health Insurance Card (EHIC) may cover a portion of your healthcare costs in Germany.

Local Support Networks
Most cities have English-speaking emergency staff, but knowing a few basic German phrases might be useful. For example, understanding how to beg for help ("Hilfe!") or stating "I need a doctor" ("Ich brauche einen Arzt") can save you time.

Keep Important Numbers Handy
Apart from emergency services, it's a good idea to carry the contact information for your country's embassy or consulate, as well as your travel

insurance provider, on hand. Consider saving these numbers to your phone or writing them down on a piece of paper in case your phone runs out of battery.

Essential Travel Apps and Websites

When I travel, I always rely on a few crucial applications and websites to make the journey easier and less stressful. Whether you're touring the bustling streets of Munich or climbing in the Bavarian Alps, these tools can help you navigate Bavaria, remain connected, and have a better overall experience. Below are some of my top recommendations:

Google Maps
I can't recommend Google Maps enough—it's my go-to program for getting around cities, finding the best routes, and discovering hidden gems in Bavaria. Whether you're walking about Munich's historic center or driving to Neuschwanstein Castle, Google Maps offers real-time traffic updates, public transportation routes, and even bicycle trails, which are ideal for those who choose a more environmentally friendly mode of transportation.

DB Navigator (Deutsche Bahn)

DB Navigator is an essential tool for traveling by train in Bavaria. Deutsche Bahn's official app provides real-time schedules for trains, buses, and trams across Germany, including Bavaria. It enables you to order tickets on the spot, check for delays, and even plan multi-leg itineraries, making it ideal for day visits or extended stays in locations such as Nuremberg or Regensburg.

Moovit
If you're taking public transportation in a larger city like Munich, Moovit is another excellent tool to help you plan your journey. It provides complete information about bus, tram, and subway lines, including arrival schedules, as well as real-time updates in case of delays. It is especially beneficial when navigating Munich's U-Bahn system, as it ensures that I always arrive on time for my train.

Uber or Lyft?
While traditional taxis are ubiquitous in Bavaria, Uber and Lyft are becoming increasingly popular, notably in Munich and Nuremberg. These applications are ideal for getting a quick trip without having to search for a taxi. The price is clear, and you can choose from a range of vehicles, making it a comfortable and dependable way to go around, particularly at night or during busy hours.

WhatsApp

Communication is essential when traveling, and WhatsApp is the greatest app for staying connected. WhatsApp works easily when reaching out to locals, organizing with travel companions, or connecting with accommodations or tour guides. Many hotels, restaurants, and even tour organizations use WhatsApp for customer service, so it's a useful app to have on your phone while visiting Bavaria.

Trip Advisor

When I'm planning a trip or looking for something to do, I go to TripAdvisor. From local restaurants to attractions and hidden secrets, this app offers evaluations and recommendations from other travelers. It's extremely handy for locating top-rated restaurants in Munich or finding off-the-beaten-path hiking trails in the Bavarian Alps. In addition, the app allows you to book tickets and make restaurant reservations directly.

Booking.com

Booking.com is one of my favorite accommodation sites. It allows me to compare hotels, hostels, and guesthouses in towns like Munich, Nuremberg, and Garmisch-Partenkirchen, and I appreciate the ability to read extensive evaluations. The app frequently offers last-minute savings and allows me to change my reservation if circumstances change. It's a lifesaver when I need to find a place to stay quickly or want to explore unique boutique hotels in the Bavarian countryside.

Google Translate
While many people in Bavaria understand English, particularly in tourist-friendly places, it's always a good idea to have Google Translate handy. The app's camera feature allows you to aim your phone at a menu or road sign and instantly translate it, which is very useful when you're in rural areas or dealing with unique Bavarian dialects.

XE Currency
Bavaria, like the rest of Germany, utilizes the Euro, but if you're coming from outside the Eurozone, XE Currency is a great tool for keeping track of exchange rates. The software allows you to instantly convert currencies, giving you a decent indication of how much you're spending, whether you're shopping in Munich or getting a snack in a little Bavarian village.

All Trails
For nature lovers and outdoor enthusiasts, AllTrails is an excellent software. Whether you're hiking in

the Bavarian Alps, strolling around Tegernsee, or simply exploring a nearby park, AllTrails offers extensive route maps, difficulty ratings, and user reviews. It's the ideal tool for identifying the best hiking sites, whether you're a beginner or an expert mountaineer.

Chapter 8: Suggested Itinerary for Bavaria

3-Day Itinerary for First-Time Visitors

If you're visiting Bavaria for the first time and want to explore the main attractions without feeling rushed, this 3-day schedule is ideal. I've created a well-balanced itinerary that allows you to visit the key sights, experience Bavarian culture, and even relax in this stunning location.

Day 1: Munich, the heart of Bavaria
Begin your Bavarian tour in Munich, the busy capital. Begin the day by visiting Marienplatz,

Munich's central center. I recommend arriving early to watch the famed Glockenspiel in operation. From there, walk through the historic alleyways to the Frauenkirche, Munich's landmark cathedral, and then explore the gorgeous Viktualienmarkt, a bustling food market.

In the afternoon, visit Nymphenburg Palace to see its spectacular Baroque buildings and expansive gardens. Afterward, enjoy a leisurely stroll in the English Garden, one of the world's largest urban parks. Don't forget to visit a beer garden for a refreshing Maß of beer.

Finish the day with dinner at Munich's iconic beer hall, the Hofbräuhaus. Enjoy typical Bavarian cuisine such as Wiener Schnitzel and Schweinebraten while taking in the boisterous environment.

Day 2: Neuschwanstein Castle & Füssen
On day two, we'll visit Neuschwanstein Castle, one of Bavaria's most recognizable attractions. Make your way to Füssen (approximately a 2-hour drive from Munich), a quaint village at the foot of the Bavarian Alps. Take a bus or a lovely trek to the castle. Spend the morning discovering the fairy-tale

edifice that inspired Disney's Sleeping Beauty Castle.

After viewing Neuschwanstein, proceed to the adjacent Hohenschwangau Castle, King Ludwig II's childhood home. In the afternoon, spend some time exploring Füssen's medieval old town and relaxing by the Forggensee Lake. You can also eat a Bavarian lunch in one of the charming local restaurants before returning to Munich.

Day 3: The Bavarian Alps and Garmisch-Partenkirchen
On your final day, discover the breathtaking Bavarian Alps. Visit Garmisch-Partenkirchen, one of the region's most popular destinations for outdoor sports. Garmisch has a variety of activities available, including hiking, skiing (in the winter), and simply enjoying the beautiful scenery.

If you visit during the warmer months, take the Zugspitze Cable Car up to Germany's highest mountain for panoramic views of the Alps. In the winter, you can go skiing or snowboarding here. If you're not a skier, the mountain trails offer plenty of tranquil treks and excellent photo possibilities.

Finish your day with a visit to the Partnach Gorge, a breathtaking natural marvel where you can take a picturesque trek amid waterfalls and spectacular rock formations. Afterward, return to Munich to recuperate before going home.

7-Day Itinerary for a Deeper Exploration of Bavaria

For those with more time and a desire to delve further into what Bavaria has to offer, this 7-day itinerary goes beyond the must-see sights and allows you to immerse yourself in the region's rich culture, history, and natural beauty.

Day 1: Arrival in Munich
Begin your journey in Munich. Spend the day at the Deutsches Museum, one of the world's largest museums of technology and science. Afterward, take a leisurely stroll through Marienplatz and explore the nearby shopping districts, such as Kaufingerstrasse. If you enjoy art, a visit to the Alte Pinakothek or Neue Pinakothek is essential.

For dinner, I propose stopping at one of Munich's famous beer gardens, such as Augustiner-Keller. Enjoy a cool beer with a pretzel and some substantial Bavarian cuisine.

Day 2: Explore the Castles and Alpine Villages

On day two, travel south to see two of Bavaria's most famous castles, Neuschwanstein and Hohenschwangau. Take a guided tour of these breathtaking landmarks to discover their outstanding interiors and environs. Afterward, enjoy a lovely drive through the Alpsee region to the charming village of Oberammergau, which is noted for its woodcarving history and exquisite painted buildings.

Day 3: Hiking through the Bavarian Alps

Take a full day to enjoy the natural splendor of the Bavarian Alps. Visit Garmisch-Partenkirchen, where you may ride the cable car to the Zugspitze or spend the day hiking in the vicinity. One of my favorite walks is the Partnach Gorge, which offers beautiful views of waterfalls, rich flora, and high cliffs.

Finish the day with a warm meal at a nearby alpine lodge, where you may try regional favorites like Käsespätzle (cheese noodles) and Bavarian roast pork.

Day 4: Nuremberg—History and Culture

Travel to Nuremberg to take a historical excursion through Bavaria's medieval heart. Visit Nuremberg Castle, the Albrecht Dürer House, and the Documentation Center Nazi Party Rally Grounds to learn about the city's significance in both medieval and modern history.

Nuremberg is particularly famed for its Christmas Market, although you may visit its numerous small shops, cafés, and restaurants all year round. Make sure to try the famed Nürnberger Bratwurst and a glass of the local Nuremberg beer.

Day 5: Explore Franconia's Wine Region
Spend day five touring the Franconian Wine Region. Franconia, in northern Bavaria, is famous for its distinctive Bocksbeutel wine bottles and exquisite white wines. Visit Bamberg, with its medieval architecture and famed smoked beer, followed by a picturesque tour of the Franconian vineyards. You can also explore Würzburg, which is home to the beautiful Würzburg Residence and the Marienberg Fortress.

Day 6: Regensburg - Medieval Charm with River Views
On day six, visit Regensburg, a UNESCO World Heritage site. Explore the well-preserved medieval

old town, which features tiny lanes, cobbled streets, and ancient structures. Visit Regensburg Cathedral, one of Germany's best Gothic monuments, and walk along the Danube River. Have dinner at a local beer hall and taste the Regensburger Wurst.

Day 7: Relax at the Bavarian Lakes
On your final day, unwind by visiting one of Bavaria's beautiful lakes. Visit Lake Tegernsee or Lake Chiemsee to relax by the water, go boating, or take a leisurely trek around the lake. For a cultural experience, visit Herrenchiemsee Palace, which was erected by King Ludwig II on an island near Lake Chiemsee.

As your adventure comes to an end, take in the peaceful beauty of the Bavarian countryside before returning to Munich for your departure.

Conclusion

As I reflect on my time in Bavaria, I can't help but be grateful for the unique events and the strong bond I've formed with this stunning place. Every minute seemed like a new adventure, whether I was exploring Munich's bustling streets, trekking the gorgeous Bavarian Alps, or immersing myself in the history and culture of Neuschwanstein Castle.

Bavaria is more than just a place; it is a mood. The warmth of a substantial lunch in a quiet beer garden, the majesty of standing before centuries-old castles, and the delight of celebrating at one of the many festivals all contribute to the region's vibrancy. Every area of Bavaria has a tale to tell, from the towns' rich histories to the natural beauty that surrounds them.

But it isn't all about the scenery. What truly made my visit memorable were the people. Bavarians are among the most friendly and inviting individuals I've met. Whether they were telling anecdotes over a glass of local beer or showing me around a hidden treasure of a community, I always felt at ease. Their joy in their background, culture, and customs shines through in everything they do, and it will stay with me long after I go.

If you decide to visit Bavaria, whether for a short trip or to explore the region more thoroughly, I recommend that you immerse yourself in its culture, history, and scenery. Enjoy the slower pace of life in the countryside, eat wonderful local cuisine, and take time to ponder on the breathtaking beauty of the Alps and lakes.

Whatever your motivation for visiting—be it the towering castles, the world-famous beer culture, or the appeal of Bavarian festivals—Bavaria will leave an impression. And who knows. You might find yourself, as I did, arranging your next trip back before you even leave.

Printed in Dunstable, United Kingdom